AUTHENTIC CHRISTIANITY AND THE LIFE OF FREEDOM

AUTHENTIC CHRISTIANITY AND THE LIFE OF FREEDOM

Expository Messages from Galatians

Michael A. Milton, Ph. D.

Wipf and Stock Publishers
Eugene, Oregon

Wipf and Stock Publishers
199 West 8th Avenue, Suite 3
Eugene OR 97401

© 2005 Michael A. Milton
Authentic Christianity and the life of Freedom:
Expository Messages from Galatians
By Michael A. Milton, Ph. D.

Unless otherwise indicated, all Scripture quotations are from The Holy Bible, English Standard Version, copyright © 2001 by Crossway Bibles, a division of Good News Publishers. Used by permission. All rights reserved.

1st edition.

ISBN: 1-59725-212-0

Dedication

To the Glory of the God of Grace, who purchased my freedom and to Aunt Eva who led me to Him.

And always for Mae, who shows me His grace in so many ways.

Contents

	Acknowledgments	i
	Introduction	iii
Chapter 1	The Gospel of Freedom	3
Chapter 2	Free to Serve	17
Chapter 3	The True Believers Declaration of Independence	31
Chapter 4	Who Is the Family of God?	45
Chapter 5	Born Free	57
Chapter 6	Practical Holiness	71
Chapter 7	The Marks of a Grace-based Christian Community	85
	Author Biography	95

Acknowledgments

All pastors know that a sermon comes not only through the exegesis of the text but the exegesis of the pastor's own soul by the Holy Spirit. These messages came as the Lord Jesus worked out His will in my own heart and life. Moreover, these messages came through the inspiration of the lives of my congregation at First Presbyterian Church of Chattanooga, Tennessee. Thank you sweet saints of God! I am humbled to be called your pastor!

Each Saturday night, in our home, I am gathered into the sweet fellowship of my wife, Mae, and our son, John Michael. I want to thank them for their encouragement to me. Each of these messages were sealed by their prayers. Thank you, my dear family. I am blessed by coming each day to a sanctuary called home.

I want to also thank our dedicated pastoral staff who support my pastorate in so many ways. Mrs. Martha Miller, my secretary, and Mrs. Joye Howard, my editor, have also contributed greatly to the gospel by multiplying and maximizing the ministry of the Word. My thanks to you.

INTRODUCTION

> St. Paul wrote this epistle because, after his departure from the Galatian churches, Jewish-Christian fanatics moved in who perverted Paul's gospel of man's free justification by faith in Christ Jesus.
>
> The world bears the Gospel a grudge because the Gospel condemns the religious wisdom of the world. Jealous for its own religious views, the world in turn charges the Gospel with being a subversive and licentious doctrine, offensive to God and man, a doctrine to be persecuted as the worst plague on earth.

So Martin Luther began his famous *Commentary on Paul's Epistle to the Galatians*. One can see, even in this introduction, that much is at stake in this book. The essence of the religion of Paul (and biblical Christianity) is justification by faith in the substitutionary work of Jesus Christ on the cross by the unfathomable grace of Almighty God toward those who believe. The defense of this doctrine in the face of a man-centered imitation makes up this letter.

The Letter to the Galatians is always in great demand because the default setting of mankind seems to be a man-centered religion that aims to placate a deity through religious ritual. In the early years of the 21st Century, we desperately need the timeless truths of this book. In the East, in places like India, the multiplicity of gods strangle the God-given potential out of millions of precious human beings. In the Middle East, either fanatical Islam or a lukewarm cultural religious devotion to it grips multitudes and causes them to give up their beloved sons to death rather than receiving a gospel where God gave His Son to us. In the West, where the gospel of grace once thundered from the pulpits of cathedrals in London, quaint chapels in Wales, mighty edifices in Boston and New Orleans, there is now a postmodern spirituality that hangs over us like the toxic fog of some diabolical chemical spill. Our generation, like others before it, must know the fresh wind of the Holy Spirit carrying the clear doctrines of grace. Our sons and daughters must live free. The postmodern alternatives to the gift of eternal and abundant life, which come from the gospel of Jesus

Christ, cannot give the freedom that we all innately crave. Only an authentic Christianity can bring a life of freedom.

What follows in this little volume is a series of messages that in some small way seeks to set forth the God-given, Christ-wrought tenets of authentic Christianity that might be used of God to stir up this fresh wind and blow out the toxic fumes of man-centered religion. These sermons were preached before the congregation of First Presbyterian Church of Chattanooga, Tennessee in 2004 by one pastor concerned about these matters in the microcosm of his congregation. If they could be used to stir up more thinking and talking about—or to feed the soul of a pastor or missionary to preach about—the gospel of grace, then the book will have met its purpose.

Sola, Scriptura—Solus Christus—Sola Gratia—Sola Fide—Soli Deo Gloria

Michael A. Milton

Pentecost 2005

"Everything is of grace in the Christian life from the very beginning to the very end."

Martyn Lloyd-Jones

"The doctrines of grace humble a man without degrading him, and exalt him without inflating him."

Charles Hodge

1

THE GOSPEL OF FREEDOM

Galatians 1:1-10

On June 6, 1944, the Supreme Commander of the Allied Forces waited for the news. When it finally came, he learned that the greatest invasion force ever assembled had taken the coast of Normandy. The French people, who are the ancient Gauls, were free, and the march to Berlin was on.

On this sixtieth anniversary of D-Day, I want to begin a summer series. It, also, is about marching to freedom—the freedom that Jesus Christ brings. The field of study will be the ancient people of Gaul who had immigrated to Asia Minor. Their region was called Galatia—the place of the Gauls.

Paul's letter to all of the churches in Galatia was an amazing marshaling forward of the powerful gospel truth in the strongest words possible in order to free the Galatians from the headlong course they were on—a course that was leading them back into bondage. Bravely taking on false teachers like the allied forces took on the Nazis in the hedgerows, Paul assaults the religion of works and advances the gospel of freedom.

We, as God's people, are "prone to wander...to leave the God I love," as Robert Robertson put it. And so across the millennia comes the authentic gospel, which always leads to the life of freedom.

> Paul, an apostle—not from men nor through man, but through Jesus Christ and God the Father, who raised him from the dead—and all the brothers who are with me, To the churches of Galatia: Grace to you and peace from God our Father and the Lord Jesus Christ, who gave himself for our sins to deliver us from the present evil age, according to the will of our God and Father, to whom be the glory forever and ever. Amen. I am astonished that you are so quickly deserting him who called you in the grace of Christ and are turning to a different gospel—not that

there is another one, but there are some who trouble you and want to distort the gospel of Christ. But even if we or an angel from heaven should preach to you a gospel contrary to the one we preached to you, let him be accursed. As we have said before, so now I say again: If anyone is preaching to you a gospel contrary to the one you received, let him be accursed. For am I now seeking the approval of man, or of God? Or am I trying to please man? If I were still trying to please man, I would not be a servant of Christ (Galatians 1:1-10).

OCCUPIED BY LEGALISM

One time my wife and I were in Paris. As you may or may not know, the French are rightfully very proud of their beautiful language and prefer that visitors not expect that the French should speak anything but French. I accepted this and brushed up on my French before our trip. While in a gift shop across from Notre Dame Cathedral, I stuttered through the broken Louisiana Cajun that I had picked up along the way and asked the lady if she had a T-shirt in my size. I struggled to communicate; and the French lady tried coaxing it out of me, using hand gestures and so forth. She would pick up on what I was trying to say; and then sensing where I was going in a sentence, she would supply the missing word or correct the mangled sentence structure. An enormous amount of energy was spent on a rather mundane matter! Finally, she directed me to the right place in the store to find the shirt I wanted. I was worn out but satisfied that I had gotten through to this Galatian woman. As I was going to the back of the store, the lady leaned over and, in perfect English, whispered to my wife, "I think it's so cute that he is trying to speak French!"

Recently relations between the French, those ancient Galatian people, and our nation have been as strained as my encounter with the gift shop sales lady in Paris. There has even been some name calling. I think of that, and I recall the words of Caesar who wrote,

> "The infirmity of the Gauls is that they are fickle in their resolves, fond of change, and not to be trusted."[1]

Another ancient writer said of the Galatians, that they were

> …Generous, impulsive, vehement…vain, fickle, and quarrelsome…[2]

---

[1] The Rev. George Barlow, *Commentary on the Epistles of St. Paul the Apostle: Galatians, Ephesians, Philippians, Colossians and 1,2 Thessalonians*, 31 vols., vol. 28, *The Preacher's Complete Homiletic Commentary* (Grand Rapids, MI: Baker Books, 2001 Reprint), 1.
[2] Ibid.

while yet another said they were

> "Frank, impetuous...eminently intelligent, but at the same time extremely changeable...."[3]

I have heard those things before on talk radio shows! But let's give them their due. The French do have great food (although they don't put enough on the plate). They have given us some unforgettable literature; they have given the world some wonderful inventions. But even more important, the French, at least those Celtic bands known as the Gauls, received a letter written by Paul that is included in the Bible. The theme of the letter is that, if you consider what happened in the Galatian church, the popular and perhaps unfair assessment of those people concerning their not staying the course of fighting for what was right was somewhat justified.

But before we make jokes about the Galatians, we need to admit that what happened to the them can, has, and continues to happen to those all over the world who are called Christians, no matter what their ancestry. Probably, the Galatian problem is present in this room today. What was the Galatian problem?

Paul himself had planted the churches in that great Roman province of Galatia. The Galatians were off to a life of freedom in Christ, but their progress in grace had been assaulted. They were being taken captive by false teachers who were luring them back into a religion of works, asking them to believe that they could please God by moralism and religious acts that supposedly would bring righteousness. The churches of Galatia were occupied by legalism. They needed to be liberated.

Peter has told us that the devil goes about like a roaring lion, ready to devour whatever prey he might find.[4] And, as that preeminent Frenchman Jean Calvin, preached to a French speaking congregation in Geneva,

> "Although our Lord Jesus Christ has confirmed to us that we have been given to him by God the Father, and that those in his care shall never perish (John 17:12), we cannot sleep, or neglect to call upon God when we consider our great need of His aid. Faith may assure us of God's unfailing love, but we also need to be aware of our own frailty, and pray for unwavering fidelity to him on our part. It is written that faith will overcome the world (1 John 5:4); nevertheless, we must still be involved in the struggle!"[5]

---

[3] Ibid.
[4] 1 Peter 5:8

Calvin was right. And throughout history the church has had to stand guard against the intrusion of legalism, of teachers and movements that propose that something other than Christ's finished work must be added in order for God to be pleased with us. Our own flesh seems to rail at the idea that salvation can be by grace alone. Our own minds seem repulsed by a gospel that says we progress in our faith by the power of the Holy Spirit, not by our own power.

The failure of the Galatians to stand firm in the face of false teaching has led them astray and is leading them back into the darkness, back into the bondage from which Christ had freed them. The letter to the Galatians is Paul's prayerful but very bold plan to liberate them again—to stop the French capitulation, if you will. In doing so, God has shown every believer what authentic Christianity is, and this alone brings freedom to living.

I draw your attention, in Galatians 1:1-10, to four authenticating proofs of the gospel and one defining proposition about the gospel.

Four Authenticating Proofs

If it's the gospel, it begins with God—not man (Galatians 1:1).

A careful investigation into this letter, as well as a careful reading of Acts 15 (the council of Jerusalem, which no doubt happened during this time), reveals that the false teachers in Galatia were making some very serious charges. First, they were saying that Paul was not an apostle of Christ. Second, they were charging that the message Paul was preaching was not the gospel. Third, they were asserting that the grace Paul was preaching would lead to licentiousness. I think of the statement of Harry Reeder at Briarwood in Birmingham: If you have not been charged with antinomianism, you probably are not preaching grace. In other words, the message of grace is dangerous.

So, right out of the boat, Paul hits the beach by answering these charges. Paul states emphatically that his apostleship came, not from men, nor through men, but through Jesus Christ and God the Father. He then speaks of all of the brethren with him. The false teachers were saying that Paul was a loose cannon. He wasn't in touch with the Jerusalem church. But Paul, appointed by Christ, was recognized by the brethren. He was an apostle. There are no more of those around. Technically, they were the men who were directly commissioned by Jesus. They were there to lay the doctrinal foundation of the church. In Ephe-

---

[5] John Calvin, *Sermons on Galatians*, trans. Kathy Childress (Edinburgh: The Banner of Truth Trust, 1997), 1.

sians Paul will say that God has called some to a particular ministry, and he mentions apostles first before moving to pastors and teachers. His intention is clear: apostles are the first. They form a ministry on which the others build.

It is equally important for us to see that Paul is establishing that God is the source of this. The Bible says that no man takes this honor to himself, and neither did Paul. This not only establishes Paul's refutation of the false teacher's charges about his apostleship, but also clearly sets forth a principle about the gospel. Authentic Christianity is not something that you do, but it is something that God has done for you. It may appear to be initiated by you, but in truth it is something that God does.

I am ashamed to say it, but I am a recovering follower of the Galatian false teachers. Before you criticize me, hear how easily it happens. I was wandering far from God. I wanted a relationship with God, and I bought into the teaching, which is propagated by so much of religion, that I could please God by doing something for him. If I carefully plotted out a path of devotion, I could actually produce a holiness which would not only cover my sin, but would also bring me the happiness that I so desperately wanted. We must be honest and say that such a plan works for a while. That was my goal and my heart's desire. So I began to produce this holiness through listening to radio teachers. Then reading certain books. Then I thought, If only I could get involved with church and even get on some boards or committees. I did all of that. But there had to be more. So, I taught Sunday school. I was feeling like somebody. I was feeling a little religious, a little holy. I figured this was answering the need in my life, covering my sins, and making me the man God wanted me to be. Deep inside I was trying to get back to the faith I had seen in my own home—the quiet, confident, sweet-spirited faith of my Aunt Eva who raised me.

Then I figured that I should really do something special for God, so not only did I teach Sunday school, but I also volunteered to take some Saturday morning classes and serve as a lay reader and then as a lay preacher. Once I filled in at a church. I looked at the word pastor on the door and felt that I must now be doing all right. Once, when a real minister couldn't be found, I was asked to open the legislature with a prayer. Well, like a game at the fair, that just rang up the points! But God had not called me to himself! They introduced me as Reverend Milton, and I ate it up. But I was no reverend, and I was not happy.

I was in the chains of religion. God had not called me to preach, but I thought I was doing God a favor! What a sham I was! What a hell I was heaping up for eternity! What a desperate condition I was in! And it showed up in every area of my life. It was not until God did the work that I understood that I had nothing to offer God but my sin and my need. It was not until I saw my sin whipping the back of Christ, my lies and my black heart placing that crown of thorns on His sacred brow, my sin-sick soul nailing Him to a cross, that I understood. It was not until I knew that He had taken my sins and that I needed His righteousness, it was not until the pure love of Jesus flooded my soul that I understood that I had nothing to offer Him.

> Jesus paid it all,
> All to Him I owe;
> Sin had left a crimson stain,
> He washed it white as snow.

This morning, my beloved, I am almost 100% certain that some who are hearing my voice have such a plan. You will make yourself holy by your own actions and then you will be happy. But it is a lie from the pit of hell! The gospel is that it starts with God, not you! The gospel is so much more satisfying, my beloved. It begins with what God does for you in Jesus Christ, not what you have to do. And if anyone here will call out to Him, He will do the work in you.

So, if it is the gospel, it will start with God, not you.

If it's the gospel, it must be of grace—not obedience (Galatians 1: 3-5).

Paul greets the Galatians in grace and peace. This is not just a throw-away line but the essence of the Christian faith. Grace brings peace to living. Religion brings bondage. And moreover, this grace was made possible by God sending His Son to give Himself for us.

Again, one of the charges against Paul was that he was preaching something that was not the truth. Paul was preaching that grace alone brings peace. The false teachers were countering that holiness comes from obedience to the law.

I once had a Holstein cow named Spot (I have told you before that I was really bad at naming animals). Spot was always figuring a way to get out of the pasture. In fact, during calving season, she always got out and had her calf somewhere in the woods. Every year Aunt Eva would tell me to go find Spot and lead her and the calf back in.

That is the way it is with the false teaching of holiness by works rather than grace producing holiness. This thing is always getting out and producing more bad doctrine. Here Paul was fencing in the truth: salvation is by grace. Grace produces peace. Religious obedience will not, cannot, produce peace in the human soul. But all over the world there are religions that are trying to please God by obedience rather than through what He has done for us. In Hindu societies, "A sati [a widow] who dies on the funeral pyre of her husband enjoys an eternal bliss in heaven [Daksa Smrti IV.18-19] [Sm. Samu p.30] [1200, p.65]."[6] Rather than eat, starving people will worship a cow in order to gain acceptance with the gods. Muslims will try to gain acceptance with Allah by bowing down to Mecca. Catholics will try to gain acceptance with God by keeping holy days. Protestants will try to gain acceptance with God by church attendance; by bragging about our independence from organized religion; by signing a temperance pledge; by not playing cards; or by telling our children, Be a good boy and God will love you.

Apart from the grace of God, every religious act is guaranteed to not only cause you to miss peace, but to become entangled in spiritual bondage.

The gospel is all about grace that leads to peace, not religious obedience.

If it's the gospel, it centers on Christ—not on religion (Galatians 1: 1-5).

Paul introduces his letter by saying that He is an apostle through Christ and that Christ came to give Himself for our sin; therefore, grace and peace flow from the center of God's gift of His Son, Jesus Christ.

In other words, if it is the gospel, it is all about Jesus. It is never about religion.

In Acts 15 we read exactly what the false teachers were saying.

> But some men came down from Judea and were teaching the brothers, "Unless you are circumcised according to custom of Moses, you cannot be saved" (Acts 15:1).

It then says that Paul and Barnabus had "no small debate with them." That means they let them have it! Their religion was not centering on Christ. The truth is that, when it was according to what God had revealed, the faith of the Old Testament was also to center on Christ. The moral law, the Levitical law, and even the theocratic law were pointing to Jesus. You could not produce holiness through anything other than faith in God's Messiah. From the earliest, when God promised a Redeemer in the presence of Adam and Eve and the devil in Genesis 3:15, it has been so.

---

[6] http://www.dalitstan.org/books/gowh/gowh5.html.

If it is the gospel, it centers on Christ. Let me ask you a question. Does your faith center on Jesus?

In our minister's prayer time this week, several of us asked prayer from each other, and it went like this: Pray for me that I will keep Christ the center; I am getting dry. You see, even ministers—especially ministers—can get clinical, can focus on the needs of people and meeting those needs, giving and giving and giving, and drift from the life-giving blood of Christ.

Our church is not about you or me. It is about Jesus Christ. Our life together is to be a life connected to the Savior. If you ever see me slipping from that centrality, you let me know because the gospel is all about Jesus.

If it's the gospel, it delivers us from sin—it does not entangle us with the things of this world (Galatians 1:4).

In Galatians 1:4 Paul says that Christ gave himself to deliver us from this present evil age. This is an indictment upon the religion of man which finds its meaning here in this age. If it is the gospel, it will deliver you.

Religion cannot deliver you. Trying to keep the law, trying to be a good boy or a good girl apart from the life of Jesus will entangle you in this world. Only Christ can truly deliver you.

When I was a kid working in a petrochemical plant in Louisiana, I watched as too much pressure built up in a tank. The regulator started spinning and the whole thing suddenly blew up.

I once saw this happen in a man's life. He was trying to regulate his life, the life of his wife and children, and even the youth group of the church he pastored. Finally, the pressure became too much. He couldn't keep it up. He wasn't the man he said he was. The religion he held proposed that you could finally make yourself holy before God. You could enjoy perfection in this life. When it blew, this man lost his wife and family as well as his ministry. He fell into deep sin and became a disgrace to himself and the church.

That is what happens. Legalism brings pressure because experience cannot equal the demands of the law. You can never keep it all. You can never be good enough. And finally it blows. And there you are, smack dab in the middle of what you had been running from through all of your religious works. Does this make sense? Paul is saying that the grace of God in Jesus, trusting in Jesus Christ alone, leaning solely on His finished work, trusting in His sacrifice for your sins, going to Him in prayer, is how you are delivered. Anything else is of this world, and it's all going to blow at one time or another.

Now, these are the four proofs. Let's give attention to the final proposition from this passage.

One Defining Proposition
Since this is the gospel, there can be no other (Galatians 1:6-10).

Galatians 1:6-10 contains some of the hardest hitting words in the Bible. Paul says that in following this false teaching, the Galatians were following another gospel. Then, in Galatians 1:7, he says what he means. Their gospel is no gospel at all. There is no other gospel than salvation offered by the grace of God and received by trusting in Christ alone. Anything else, even if it were to come from an angel, is *anathema*, to use the Greek word that Paul uses. It is accursed. To use the language of Steve Brown, "it smells like smoke." Just to make sure they hear him, Paul repeats it again in Galatians 1:9; therefore, I should as well.

> As we have said before, so now I say again: If anyone is preaching to you a gospel contrary to the one you received, let him be accursed (Galatians 1:9).

CONCLUSION

I want to make sure you see the way this magnificent appeal from Paul ends.

Tom Brokaw wrote *The Greatest Generation*, a fine book, the title of which has become part of our language describing the generation that fought in World War II. Last night he talked about one of the men of that generation: Ronald Reagan, who died yesterday. Brokaw recalled that on this day twenty years ago, President Ronald Wilson Reagan stood on the shores of Normandy and spoke to the Army Rangers who had taken Pointe du Hoc on D-Day. Brokaw said that all of the reporters there knew they were witnessing what he called "one of the greatest American speeches ever given." Last night, in the midst of reflecting on President Reagan, on D-Day, and on what God has for us in His Word, my swirling thoughts landed on these lines from that speech. Standing on the wind-swept cliffs of Normandy, with the beaches behind him and the veterans of that battle around him, President Reagan said,

> These are the men who took the cliffs. These are the champions who helped free a continent. These are the heroes who helped end a war.

> Gentlemen, I look at you and I think of the words of Stephen Spender's poem. You are men who in your 'lives fought for life…and left the vivid air signed with your honor'…
>
> Forty summers have passed since the battle that you fought here. You were young the day you took these cliffs; some of you were hardly more than boys, with the deepest joys of life before you. Yet, you risked everything here. Why? Why did you do it? What impelled you to put aside the instinct for self-preservation and risk your lives to take these cliffs? What inspired all the men of the armies that met here? We look at you, and somehow we know the answer. It was faith and belief; it was loyalty and love.[7]

He was absolutely right, of course. Faith and belief, loyalty and love motivated men to become, in a sense, slaves to freedom.

In Galatians 1:10, Paul sums up grace and answers his critics. In a letter that is all about how Jesus Christ brings freedom, he says that he is a servant, a *doulos* in the Greek, a virtual slave.

When you receive the freedom that Jesus offers, it will produce a heart that says, I want to give my all to You, Lord. I want to be your *doulos*. I want to give my life away for You, O Christ. I want to give my life away for those who have never heard the gospel. I want to be a slave to others for your sake, O Christ.

And thus grace produces what legalism cannot: a heart for God and a heart for others, motivated by love.

How the world needs such a grace awakening today. How the shores of our own lives need this grace invasion today. We would be so much happier—and so free.

---

[7] The entire speech may be found at
http://www.townhall.com/hall_of_fame/reagan/speech/normandy.html.

Questions for Reflection

1. How is legalism different from obedience to Christ?

2. In this first chapter, I say, "I am ashamed to say it, but I am a recovering follower of the Galatian false teachers. Before you criticize me, hear how easily it happens." How can true believers fall prey to the "Galatian problem"?

3. Can trusting in God's grace alone for salvation lead to sin? How or how not? Is grace so dangerous that we should minimize its message?

4. How does a follower of Jesus Christ get entangled again in sin? What is suggested in Galatians to keep us from falling into sin?

5. In what ways does the world need a grace awakening today? In what areas of life (parenting, relationship with your spouse, relationship with other Christians) do you need a grace awakening?

6. In what ways does the doctrine of salvation by God's grace alone impact daily living?

7. In what ways does it impact your happiness?

Prayer

Lord Jesus—the King of Love, Your life and Your death opened the way for me to come to know abundant and eternal life. I need to rely on your grace alone. Help me to be weaned from the tendency to relate to you and others through performance. Help me to receive a fresh infusion of Your Spirit that I may be led to place my hands in the velvet chains of the Gospel and live as a slave to Your grace! I pray in Your Name O Lord.

Amen.

> "It costs God nothing, so far as we know, to create nice things; but to convert rebellious wills cost Him crucifixion."
>
> C. S. Lewis

> "John Newton, Clerk, once an infidel and libertine, a servant of slaves in Africa, was, by the rich mercy of our Lord and Savior Jesus Christ, preserved, restored, pardoned, and appointed to preach the faith he had long labored to destroy."
>
> The tombstone of John Newton
Anglican minister and author of "Amazing Grace"

2

FREE TO SERVE

Galatians 1:11-24

Not long ago I read about the trend for parents to try to get their children into just the right pre-school so that they could get into the right grammar school, which would place them at the top of the list to get into the right middle school, and hopefully, the best prep school in order to get a shot a the best college. Thinking long term, some are checking on what advantages might get them into the best grad school!

That is a ridiculous extreme, I think, but it shows just how much emphasis our society places on credentials.

What are the credentials to serve God?

> For I would have you know, brothers, that the gospel that was preached by me is not man's gospel. For I did not receive it from any man, nor was I taught it, but I received it through a revelation of Jesus Christ. For you have heard of my former life in Judaism, how I persecuted the church of God violently and tried to destroy it. And I was advancing in Judaism beyond many of my own age among my people, so extremely zealous was I for the traditions of my fathers. But when he who had set me apart before I was born, and who called me by his grace, was pleased to reveal his Son to me, in order that I might preach him among the Gentiles, I did not immediately consult with anyone; nor did I go up to Jerusalem to those who were apostles before me, but I went away into Arabia, and returned again to Damascus. Then after three years I went up to Jerusalem to visit Cephas and remained with him fifteen days. But I saw none of the other apostles except James the Lord's brother. (In what I am writing to you, before God, I do not lie!) Then I went into the regions of Syria and Cilicia. And I was still unknown in person to the churches of Judea that are in Christ. They only were hearing it said, "He who used to persecute us is now

preaching the faith he once tried to destroy." And they glorified God because of me (Galatians 1:11-24).

I Just Can't

I think that some of the saddest words ever strung together in the English language are, I just can't.

Yesterday, Sgt. Simpson said it. Sgt. Simpson is from Rome, Georgia, and has been in the Army or the Army Reserves since the early 1970s. He came into my office at the Reserve unit, and we talked about some things that needed to happen at the unit. But then, as often happens in my office, the subject changed. He told me about how he felt he was just not qualified to serve as an officer in his local church. I said, "Tell me about it." "Well, Chaplain, I don't think a man who has killed other men should serve the Lord. I am not worthy." When he said that he had killed other men, I knew I was dealing with another Vietnam Vet. I have heard it before. "Tell me about it" I said. He never sat down but just talked and talked and talked. He told me that he was a sniper in Vietnam. He had been lowered into North Vietnam in what he called his "black pajamas" with his M-16. His job was to kill the enemy, and he was successful in his mission. When he came into my office, I had been working on this sermon. I began to feel that God had led this man into my office to clarify in my heart what this sermon was all about. Here was a man who was telling me, Because of my past…I just can't serve God. I sought to show him what I would preach today. But he said, "Thank you, Chaplain. But I can never serve God in that way. I am not qualified." Pray that I will have more time with Sgt. Simpson.

Sgt. Simpson prayed with me and was leaving my office, so I turned my face again to the computer screen on my lap and the Bible on my desk. Literally before I could strike a key, another soldier showed up at the door. "Chaplain? I hate to interrupt…." I now knew this was not an interruption but a divine appointment. I told him that he was not an interruption and that he should come in. He said, "You know, I asked you to pray for me this morning at chapel." "Yes," I said. "Well, Sir, I need to talk." Sgt. Becker went on to tell me that the divorce was final. He told me that his wife had left him and moved in with another man. Their daughter, Meagan, was living with him. I asked about his church home. He told me, "This is the problem. You see, Chaplain, since I became a single dad and my little twelve-year-old daughter is now a child of divorced parents, even old friends and Sunday school teachers are treating us in a different way. This week, my daughter told that she wouldn't go back to church again. 'It is too much pressure. I'm no longer good enough. I can't go back...I just can't, Dad.'"

By then I knew what God wanted to address in our lives from Galatians 1:11-24. Today the Lord wants to speak to real people with real life situations that they think are preventing them from service. I am thinking of the businessman who has known failure and who has been given another opportunity but who says, I just can't. I am thinking of the young man in college who has failed and dropped out and is invited to return to school, but is saying, I just can't. I am thinking of the child whose family has had to move around, who must face yet another school and walk into a new group of kids all staring at her—and she says, I just can't. So many people want to be free to live again, to serve again, to be used again. But they just can't.

People were likely saying that about Paul. With his past, there was no way he could serve Jesus Christ. Gresham Machen, the giant New Testament scholar and preacher of Princeton and later Westminster, believes that "each historical event" in Galatians "seems to be related in order to answer a specific argument raised by Paul's opponents...".[1] The false teachers not only questioned Paul's apostleship and challenged Paul's message, but they also sought to use Paul's past to say that he was not qualified to serve. But Paul shows that through the gospel, he has been qualified—freed—to serve God. Now this passage does not discuss gifts; Paul will deal with that in Romans 12 and in 1 Corinthians 12. But here, through the telling of how God's story intercepted Paul's story and the two became one, we see how every true believer is freed to serve the Lord.

In this passage Paul shares five core convictions about our freedom to serve.

Believers Are Freed to Serve through the Supernatural Gospel of God (Galataíns 1:11)

Paul makes it abundantly clear that he can serve the Lord because this gospel came from God and not from man. Indeed, in the Greek the words he uses to introduce his argument begins with *gnorizo*. The word means "to make clear" or "to clarify."[2] I used to have a company commander in Navy Boot Camp who would say, "Have I made myself perfectly clear to you, son?" He would say that to emphasize or underscore what he wanted me to know. He always got

---

[1] Gresham Machen, *The Origin of Paul's Religion* (1921, Reprint, Grand Rapids: Eerdmans, 1947), pp. 85, 86 as cited in *Expositor's Bible Commentary* (Grand Rapids, MI: Zondervan Publishing House, 1976), Vol 10, 436.
[2] *Expositor's Bible Commentary* (Grand Rapids, MI: Zondervan Publishing House, 1976), Vol 10, 431.

through, by the way. And here Paul is saying, Let me make myself perfectly clear about my ordination credentials. I am able to serve God because this gospel that came to me was not something made up by any man. This came from God.

This is critical to the rest of the argument. If Paul's message is from man or is made up by man, then he is not free to serve God. He has no authority and no power in his ministry. In Romans, where he is going to deliver some of the loftiest teaching about God and the gospel ever put forward in history, Paul begins by calling what he is about to teach, "the gospel of God."[3] His credentials to serve come from that power.

You will recall that the common people were attracted to Jesus Christ because they said he spoke as one having authority, not—and I emphasize—not like the Pharisees. The truth is that the Pharisees were authorized, legalized, sanitized, homogenized, and everything else by man, but not by God. You can put every seal of approval, every degree, every title, and every credential you want on a man; but if his ministry is not grounded in the gospel of God, there is no power. You can confirm, bless, baptize, ordain, and commission as much as you want; but if it is not grounded in the gospel of God, there is no real power from God. It is of man; and that has no authority, no eternal value, no lasting ministry.

But if Christ has freed you through the gospel of His grace, then, my beloved, that is the first and most powerful credential you have to serve the Lord.

> Therefore, if anyone is in Christ, he is a new creation; the old has gone, the new has come! (2 Corinthians 5:17, NIV).

If it is of man, then three strikes and you are out. One bad move and its over. But if you are staking your life on the gospel of Jesus, be sure you know that God forgives, restores, and renews. You can serve God because this gospel is of God and not of man.

Paul then continues his argument.

Believers Are Freed to Serve through a Personal Relationship with Christ (Galatians 1:12)

Paul began by pointing to the supernatural gospel of God as the ground for his qualification, but then he moves to a personal contact with Christ as yet another credential. Paul is saying that he was not taught the gospel by men, but it came to him directly from Christ. Now this is not an indictment against teach-

---
[3] Romans 1:1

ing or sitting under teaching. Teaching from ministers of the gospel and other Bible teachers is the ordinary way we grow in the truth of God's Word. Thus, Paul tells Timothy to rightly divide the word of truth so that he can minister the Word to others.[4] Jesus said, "Feed my sheep."[5] Paul is establishing that he became an apostle through personal contact with the risen Christ. This was his credential. He did not gain what he had from Peter or James or anyone else.

In 1 Corinthians 15:1, 3 Paul declares the same thing he says here: Jesus Christ personally committed to him the truths of the gospel and now he is teaching this to others.

> Now I would remind you, brothers, of the gospel I preached to you, which you received, in which you stand (1 Corinthians 15:1).

> For I delivered to you as of first importance what I also received: that Christ died for our sins in accordance with the Scriptures (1 Corinthians 15:3).

The power for our lives in this passage is that through a personal calling from Christ, we are freed to serve Him; liberated from our past lives to be used of Him; and our power comes not only from the grace of God, but also from getting this grace personally from Jesus. No, we don't get it like the apostles who received it face-to-face from Jesus Christ, but we do get it personally.

I still think one of the greatest ideas that has ever reached the mind of man is that we can know God, our creator, personally. When we do, our lives are transformed forever. His purposes and plans begin to lovingly overwhelm us, and we are caught up into something that is greater than ourselves.

Last Sunday night we offered a course in helping people share their personal testimonies. This remains the greatest tool I know of in sharing the gospel with others. One person relating what life was like before Christ, how they received Christ, and the difference that Christ now makes in their life is a powerful force for releasing others from the bondage that sin creates.

I wonder how many would pray right now, Lord, use me this week to share with another person my testimony of your personal touch on my life. I wonder how many, if you were really honest, might say, I have never known Christ in this way. Jesus says,

> "I have come that they may have life, and that they may have it more abundantly".(John 10:10b, NKJV).

---

[4] 2 Timothy 2:15
[5] John 21:17

He tells us that we must abide in Him to have true life.[6] And you can have that today by believing in Him, inviting Him to live in your life, and getting to know Him in His Word.

Believers Are Freed to Serve through the Providential Calling of God (Galatians 1:15-16)

Paul shows how the gospel is all about God and His sovereign calling on his life. His credentials, his freedom to serve and to teach and to minister, are grounded in the secret council of God Himself.

> But when he who had set me apart before I was born, and who called me by his grace, was pleased to reveal his Son to me, in order that I might preach him among the Gentiles, I did not immediately consult with anyone (Galatians 1:15,16).

The truth of God's electing love may seem to be deep and mysterious; such an acknowledgment in your life requires utmost surrender to God, reveals utmost death of self, reassigns utmost credit to God. But it also releases utmost power for living and for service.

You will remember that Jeremiah was commissioned to serve God by calling Jerusalem to repentance and warning of the coming judgment. This was a big job for what Jeremiah thought was a young fellow. So God encouraged him and stirred up courage by saying to him,

> "Before I formed you in the womb I knew you, and before you were born I consecrated you; I appointed you a prophet to the nations" (Jeremiah 1:5).

Jesus told His disciples,

> "You did not choose me, but I chose you and appointed you that you should go and bear fruit and that your fruit should abide, so that whatever you ask the Father in my name, he may give it to you" (John 15:16).

Why did the Lord say this to Jeremiah? Why did the Lord say this to the disciples? For theological speculation? No, for the same reason Paul is clinging to it now. God has called him and that gives power.

The realization and recognition that the sovereign God of the universe had me on His heart before I was born, had me on His heart before He created the world, sent His only begotten Son to live for me and die for me, sent His Spirit to

---
[6] John 15:1-11

woe me into His kingdom and cause me to be His son—that gives me power. This was the conviction of Paul against all the opposition: I am called by God.

At a community gathering last Friday I had the opportunity to share some reflections on the life of Ronald Reagan. As I did, I reminded the audience that from the time he was a child, Reagan was grounded in staunch Calvinistic, old-fashioned Bible teaching by his mother, Nelle. Over and over again she taught him the central truth that God had a plan for that boy's life, that he had to do God's will, and that apart from God he could not know God's blessing. I think that this truth was at the heart of his success. Every obstacle he faced—personal pain from his poverty-stricken childhood; the alcoholism of his father; the personal failures he faced as an adult; the crises he faced in the political world; and as he was shot, as he held the weight of the world on his shoulders at Reykjavik when he walked away from negotiations with the Soviet Union over his convictions which others didn't agree with, and as he faced Alzheimer's disease—he faced them trusting in the will of God. And even as they laid his body to rest in the Simi Valley and the sunset cast a golden glow over the whole scene, the testimonies of his own children and of his pastor told it all: this man was called of God and his faith in the God who ordains, who rules and overrules, saw him through even the last trial of his life.

There is power in that, my friends. You say, Well, I don't understand how this works. If God did the choosing, then where is my free will? Friends, don't forget the first point: this is the gospel of God. This is not taught by man; otherwise, you would understand it completely. But then again, it would have no power to save you or others. Just suffice it to trust in the Word of God that whoever calls upon the name of the Lord will be saved. When you do that, God is waiting to let you know, like a good father watching a toddler walk, that He was there all along. Without violating the freedom He gave you one iota, He was totally responsible for your coming to Him.

And that gives power in your life and freedom to living.

Believers Are Freed to Serve Without Any Other Qualifications (Galatians 1:13-22)

In the text, Paul launches into a mini-biography. It includes, not a strict chronology, but a series of events in his life:
- His devotion and zeal for rabbinical Judaism
- His persecution of believers in Christ
- His sovereign election in God, which we just spoke of

- His calling to preach the gospel of Jesus Christ
- His wilderness journey to Arabia and return to Damascus
- His visit to Jerusalem three years later and then his ministry in Syria and Cilicia

Now I draw your attention to the heart of this particular section:

> And I was still unknown in person to the churches of Judea that are in Christ. They only were hearing it said... (Galatians 1:22, 23).

Again, this man's reputation as a minister has been assaulted. Instead of naming the names of all who would have known him, he admits that no one knows him. Paul counted every human achievement as rubbish. He is also saying that though he was a fast-track clergyman on his way up, that was no qualification. His only qualification was Christ.

One of my favorite characters in the Bible is Amos, the country-preacher-come-to-town. He was called by God to go into the Northern Kingdom of Israel and to go right to the top. He was to preach to King Jeroboam of Israel. The problem was that Jeroboam had this slick clergyman named Amaziah, the priest of Bethel. There are many ministers like Amaziah today. They are professional clergymen who have all the right degrees, all the right words, and all the right connections. They lack in only one thing: the Word of God and the Spirit of God! Like Amaziah, they go around hob-knobbing with all of the other religious leaders, even those who don't name the name of Christ, After all, we must be ecumenical, they say. Well, here came old Amos. So Amaziah told the King all about Amos and how he was just not getting along well with the other clergy. He told him, in fact, that Amos was plotting against the king and that his speeches would destroy the country. Good Bible preaching generally gets that kind of reputation. Well, there was an encounter, and Amaziah, the slick cleric, met with Amos, the country preacher. Amaziah was indignant over the presence of that southern fig farmer, lay preacher in the royal court. And we read,

> And Amaziah said to Amos, "O seer, go, flee away to the land of Judah, earn your bread there, and prophesy there; but never again prophesy at Bethel, for it is the king's sanctuary, and it is a temple of the kingdom" (Amos 7:12, 13, NRSV).

Amos answered Amaziah,

> Then Amos answered Amaziah, "I am no prophet, nor a prophet's son; but I am a herdsman, and a dresser of sycamore trees, and the LORD took me from following the flock, and the LORD said to me,

> 'Go, prophesy to my people Israel.' Now therefore hear the word of the LORD. You say, 'Do not prophesy against Israel, and do not preach against the house of Isaac.' Therefore thus says the LORD:" (Amos 7:14-17a, NRSV).

For Amos, the freedom for service came from no qualification he had, but only from the fact that God had called him.

Sometimes people think that to be qualified to serve God they need to have the right connections with men. Paul knew none of that. And neither should we. We don't need any qualification other than that Christ saved us, and any disqualification we might have is covered by the blood of Christ. When people are in need, they don't look for plaques on a wall, but for a Savior on our lips, and the Lord in our hearts. What power comes to the man or woman, boy or girl, who knows that the only qualification they need to serve God is the grace of God that Jesus Christ won for them through His righteous, perfect sacrifice for our sins.

Believers Who Are Freed to Serve, Bring Glory to God (Galations 1:23-24)

I love the end of this passage. All they knew of Paul was that the one who once sought to destroy the gospel is now preaching it. I am almost moved to tears by this phrase:

> And they praised God because of me (Galatians 1:24, NIV).

He was in wonder over the grace of God. The blasphemer, the persecutor, the legalist, the hypocrite was now brining glory to God. And they were saying that he couldn't serve.

Paul's story is his credentials, for in saving him Christ brought honor to Himself. Thus, Paul would write,

> I thank him who has given me strength, Christ Jesus our Lord, because he judged me faithful, appointing me to his service, though formerly I was a blasphemer, persecutor, and insolent opponent. But I received mercy because I had acted ignorantly in unbelief, and the grace of our Lord overflowed for me with the faith and love that are in Christ Jesus. The saying is trustworthy and deserving of full acceptance, that Christ Jesus came into the world to save sinners, of whom I am the foremost. But I received mercy for this reason, that in me, as the foremost, Jesus

> Christ might display his perfect patience as an example to those who were to believe in him for eternal life (1 Timothy 1:12-16).

He would also write,

> But God chose the foolish things of the world to shame the wise; God chose the weak things of the world to shame the strong (1 Corinthians 1:27, NIV).
>
> For when I am weak, then I am strong (2 Corinthians 12:10b, NIV).

Those whom God crushes most, He uses best. So you see, your life is going to bring glory to God. The greater the pain and heartache in your life, the greater God's grace is going to rush through your life. You say, I've been cut; there are deep ravines cut in my life. Well, deep grace will run through your life.

In a few weeks my old pastor, Robert E. Baxter, will preach here. There was a day when I felt that God was calling me to the ministry of the gospel to preach, to pastor His flock, to share His grace with others. But I looked back over my life; and I felt the landscape was too littered with mistakes, too crowded with pain, too marred by sin. I knew Christ had saved me, but could He use me? And Pastor Bob said to me, "Mike, how God saved you and healed you will always be your strength. It gives God all the glory. God is calling you. You are broken, but we all are broken in one way or another. Go and minister. And minister out of your weakness."

Do you know what he was telling me? Pastor Bob was saying that in a world of "You can't," God is saying, "You can."

That is what I told Sgt. Simpson: Sgt., you can serve God. And that is what I told Sgt. Becker: Sgt., you can go on with your life. And that is what I would love to tell his little twelve-year-old daughter: Honey, you can do it; you can serve the Lord because you are accepted through Jesus and, thus, you are accepted by God. That is what God says to the failed businessman and the failed husband and, yes, to the worst and most vile sinner here today. In Christ, you can. You can live again. You can go on. You can be saved. And that is what I say to you. In Jesus Christ and in His gospel, He qualifies you for new life and service and new hope for living through His righteousness. That is what grace is all about. Whatever you have to offer him, my beloved, offer it to him. Christ will save you. Christ will forgive you. Christ will heal you. Christ will help you to forgive others. Though Jesus Christ, you can.

Questions for Reflection

1. What things hinder us from serving God?

2. In what ways do you serve God out of fear or duty only?

3. How can we reclaim joy in our service to God? Is it possible to honestly serve God without a sense of joy and freedom? Have you seen it done?

4. Think about someone in your life who has been a model of Christian service to you. Were they essentially happy or sad? In what ways would you want to imitate them?

5. What is the relationship of grace to working in your church?

6. How do you believe God has called you to represent Him today?

7. What qualifications do you bring for your service to God?

Prayer

Father of all mercy, who showed us service and love wed into one through Your Son, Jesus Christ, help me to move from fear to joy in my service. Open my heart to see new ways that I may serve you. Release me from service as duty, and lead me to serve out of an overflow of your grace in my life. In Jesus' name.

Amen.

"The law demands what it cannot give; grace gives all it demands."

Blaise Pascal

"The law discovers the disease. The gospel gives the remedy."

Martin Luther

3

THE TRUE BELIEVER'S DECLARATION OF INDEPENDENCE

Leviticus 25:10; Galatians 2:15-21

The famous words were read:

> We hold these truths to be self-evident, that all men are created equal, that they are endowed by their Creator with certain inalienable Rights; that among these are Life, Liberty, and the pursuit of Happiness. ...

> ...And for the support of this Declaration, with a firm reliance upon the protection of divine Providence, we mutually pledge to each other our Lives, our Fortunes, and our sacred Honor.

And the Liberty Bell was rung.

But did you know that on that bell are the words of Scripture that planted a divine idea of freedom in the hearts of so many of those who devised those words? Inscribed on the Liberty Bell are the words of Leviticus 25:10:

> And ye shall hallow the fiftieth year, and proclaim liberty throughout all the land unto all the inhabitants thereof: it shall be a jubilee unto you; and ye shall return every man unto his possession, and ye shall return every man unto his family. (Leviticus 25:10, KJV)

The Year of Jubilee was just one of the many ways God went about telling us that what our hearts intuitively long for is what He has prepared for us: freedom. We should always be vigilant to protect that freedom. That is what is happening with Paul in Galatians 1. For Paul, the Year of Jubilee is here. It is Jesus. Nothing should cause us to go back, nothing should shake our resolve to stand up for that freedom because that freedom was won by the blood of Jesus

Christ. And it belongs to everyone who calls on the name of the Lord, regardless of race or past sin.

> We ourselves are Jews by birth and not Gentile sinners; yet we know that a person is not justified by works of the law but through faith in Jesus Christ, so we also have believed in Christ Jesus, in order to be justified by faith in Christ and not by works of the law, because by works of the law no one will be justified. But if, in our endeavor to be justified in Christ, we too were found to be sinners, is Christ then a servant of sin? Certainly not! For if I rebuild what I tore down, I prove myself to be a transgressor. For through the law I died to the law, so that I might live to God. I have been crucified with Christ. It is no longer I who live, but Christ who lives in me. And the life I now live in the flesh I live by faith in the Son of God, who loved me and gave himself for me. I do not nullify the grace of God, for if justification were through the law, then Christ died for no purpose (Galatians 2:15-21).

This morning, lets ring out the truth about God's grace as we consider "The True Believer's Declaration of Independence."

THE BATTLE MUST BE WON IN THE HEART

Before any battle can be won on the field, a battle must be won in the minds and hearts of the people.

On March 23, 1775, that battle had to be won in the Virginia House of Burgesses in Williamsburg, Virginia. The man who would become known as the Voice of the Revolution, Patrick Henry, called his own people to see the choice they had before them. I know you are familiar the last line, but today I have reason to give you the last paragraph of that call.

> Gentlemen may cry, Peace, Peace—but there is no peace. The war is actually begun! The next gale that sweeps from the north will bring to our ears the clash of resounding arms! Our brethren are already in the field! Why stand we here idle? What is it that gentlemen wish? What would they have? Is life so dear, or peace so sweet, as to be purchased at the price of chains and slavery? Forbid it, Almighty God! I know not what course others may take; but as for me, give me liberty or give me death![1]

The remarkable thrust of that speech was to stir his fellow countrymen to see what was at stake. For want of peace, they would become slaves. Before there

---

[1] Patrick Henry, *Give Me Liberty or Give Me Death* [World Wide Web] (Libertyonline, March 23, 1775 [cited July 3 2004]); available from http://libertyonline.hypermall.com/henry-liberty.html.

could be freedom in America, there had to be a willingness in the hearts of Americans to die for freedom.

The churches of Galatia were not to that point yet. Perhaps the Galatian pastors at that time thought, Can't we just live in peace? Let's just go along with what others are saying about forcing converts to keep Jewish law to be saved.

That had been the idea for a long time. But that was not the gospel, and it was not the freedom that God had planned for the world. It was even a distortion and a misuse of the law. Law was never given without love, but that had been compromised as well. Sadly, even Peter and Barnabas became apathetic and did not stand up. Before the enemy could be addressed, as it were, the church had to be corrected. All future world missions, all future evangelism, all future understanding of the Christian faith depended upon the outcome of this debate.

But one man, a Patrick Henry of his day, stood up.

In Galatians 2 Paul recounts this climactic moment in church history. It was a struggle for freedom. The Apostle Paul relates how this struggle for freedom in Christ brought him to Jerusalem where he fought for grace. He tells about how this struggle for grace even caused him to confront Peter face-to-face; how even Barnabas, his companion in the ministry, had given in to the false teachers who were demanding religious ritual as a condition for earning God's favor. Paul withstood false teachers without and wavering friends within in order to establish the gospel that a man is justified before God ONLY through faith in Jesus Christ. This story of how he defended grace builds until at last it becomes very personal and Paul delivers his climactic and divinely wrought oratory:

> I have been crucified with Christ. It is no longer I who live, but Christ who lives in me. And the life I now live in the flesh I live by faith in the Son of God, who loved me and gave himself for me. I do not nullify the grace of God, for if justification were through the law, then Christ died for no purpose (Galatians 2:20-21).

These words are more compelling than Patrick Henry facing his fainting friends and proclaiming, "Give me liberty or give me death!"[2] This is more convicting than Winston Churchill challenging the spirit of appeasement lurking in the British nation and announcing, "I have nothing to offer but blood, toil, tears and sweat."[3] This is more critical than Ronald Reagan's face-off with

---

[2] See http://libertyonline.hypermall.com/henry-liberty.html.
[3] See http://www.winstonchurchill.org/i4a/pages/index.cfm?pageid=388.

an "evil empire" and a West who said that we would have to learn to live with Communism, demanding, "Mr. Gorbachev, tear down this wall!"[4]

These gripping words in Galatians 2:20, 21 are inspired of the Holy Spirit and spoken through Paul to the church through all the ages. These words must be liken to the words of Joshua:

> "... choose you this day whom ye will serve; whether the gods which your fathers served that were on the other side of the flood, or the gods of the Amorites, in whose land ye dwell: but as for me and my house, we will serve the LORD" (Joshua 24:15, KJV).

These words are like the words of the prophet Elijah, who in 1 Kings 18:21 went before the people and said,

> "How long will you waver between two opinions? If the LORD is God, follow him; but if Baal is God, follow him" (1 Kings 18:21, NIV).

This is the song of an unshackled soul; this is the sacred flame of a man on fire for Christ. This is what the great Australian scholar Leon Morris called "Paul's Charter of Freedom."[5] Today I want to call it "The True Believer's Declaration of Independence."

There are three articles of this declaration that are vital to every person hearing this. I want to put it in the simplest form possible and then treat each one.

His Death Saves Me.
I have been crucified with Christ… (Galatians 2:20).

Before we unpack this passage, we need to think about the fact that when Paul burst forth in this declaration, there were common assumptions in this debate which may be lost today and which need clarification. At that time, both Paul and the false teachers understood that there is a holy God who requires perfection and that there is sinful man who has rebelled against God, is born in sin, and is separated from God. Thus, man needed to be justified before this God. The false teachers were saying that justification—getting right with God—is accomplished through obedience to the law. Paul says, No, it is based on obedience to the gospel only. It is not what we do but what God has done in Christ. The problem is this: modern man, we are told, does not necessarily think in these categories.

---

[4] See http://www.nationalreview.com/document/reagan_berlin200406070934.asp.
[5] Leon Morris, *Galatians: Paul's Charter of Christian Freedom* (Downer's Grove, IL: InterVarsity Press, 1996).

The True Believer's Declaration of Independence · Chapter 3

Robert Bellah in his *Habits of the Human Heart: Individualism and Commitment in American Life* writes:

> In the absence of any objectifiable criteria of right and wrong, good or evil, the self and its feelings become our only moral guide.[6]

Or in the words of Mark Twain, "something moral is something you feel good after." Of course, the opposite of this is that if you feel bad about it, this must be immoral. You can see how problematic this becomes when thinking in terms of moral absolutes. It is all relative. This subjectivism, this moral relativity, this every-man-does-what-is-right-in-his-own–eyes, we are told, is the current situation in the human mind in the postmodern west. I think the New Testament scholar Scott McKnight was, thus, right when he remarked,

> It is my contention that until our society awakens morally, it will be difficult to apply the doctrine of justification.[7]

Justification, the defining doctrine of Christianity, is lost if there is no right or wrong, if there is no God who is holy and whose wrath against sin must be assuaged. Without this basic understanding, the question becomes, What is the use of even dealing with this passage? We have no common understanding of sin and God and the need to be justified before this God. What are we to do? Is the Bible relevant at this point?

I believe that since it is the inerrant and infallible Word of God, it is always relevant. It speaks into the very soul of man and destroys his presuppositions and establishes the truth that man is alienated from his God. Today we don't need more critique of culture; we need more straight *kerygma*, preaching of the Bible! We don't need more psychoanalyzing of society; we need more study of Scripture. Christians need to call our generation to see that there is a God and that He has spoken and declared our righteousness as filthy rags. We need a theology that emphasizes the plight of man as well as the power of God. And all of that comes from the Bible. I for one feel perfectly safe and on good ground to begin with a presupposition that

> ...the word of God is living and active. Sharper than any double-edged sword, it penetrates even to dividing soul and spirit, joints

---

[6] R. Bellah, et al., *Habits of the Heart, Individualism and Commitment in American Life* (San Francisco: Harper and Row,1986, 76 as cited in Scott McKnight, *Galatians, The NIV Application Commentary* (Grand Rapids: Zondervan, 1995).127-128.
[7] Ibid.

and marrow; it judges the thoughts and attitudes of the heart (Hebrews 4:12, NIV).

If we admit the power of God's Word over man and assume that men are sinners and need to be put right with God, the question becomes, How can we get right with this holy God? That takes us back to the context of this passage.

If Christianity was a fulfillment of the ancient promises made to Abraham, Isaac, and Jacob, and if they were now moving out to the entire earth, the question came, Since in the past, a foreigner who wanted to become a part of Israel had to undergo circumcision, doesn't it still stand? Paul—the Hebrew of Hebrews, one schooled in the finest tradition of Judaic law, but one who had been touched by the grace of God in Christ—said, No; man was never justified by works of the law. Paul was not throwing away the law and introducing antinomianism, moral anarchy; and that is the point of Galatians 2:17, "does that mean that Christ promotes sin?" (NIV). Of course not. Paul is not talking about the role of the moral law, the ten commandments, in a person's life. He is simply asserting that the moral law, the ceremonial law, or any tradition based on those laws cannot justify a person before God.

What does? Only the cross. Only the sacrificial death of Jesus Christ can atone for sin. And here Paul makes it very personal. "I have been crucified with Christ." Of course, Paul did not mean that he (Paul) had gone to Calvary to die. Paul is saying that at Calvary Christ died to save sinners vicariously; He went for Paul. What happened on the cross was done for Paul and, thus, Paul was there.

This is what Isaiah 53 was talking about when that great chapter pictures Jesus on the cross:

> But he was pierced for our transgressions,
> he was crushed for our iniquities;the punishment that brought us peace
> was upon him,
> and by his wounds we are healed (Isaiah 53:5, NIV).
>
> We all, like sheep, have gone astray,
> each of us has turned to his own way;
> and the LORD has laid on him
> the iniquity of us all (Isaiah 53:6, NIV).
>
> For he bore the sin of many,
> and made intercession for the transgressors (Isaiah 53:12b, NIV)

Paul is declaring that on the cross his sins were put to death in Christ. The great Puritan expositor John Owen called it "the death of death in the death of Christ." In a book of the same title, John Owen wrote,

> The sum of all is,—the death and blood-shedding of Jesus Christ hath wrought, and doth effectually procure... grace here and glory hereafter.[8]

But there is more to what Paul is saying. He is getting at what Jesus was telling Nicodemus:

> ..."I tell you the truth, no one can see the kingdom of God unless he is born again" (John 3:3, NIV)

This new birth begins with death. Thus, Bonhoeffer was exactly right when he said in the *Cost of Discipleship*, "Jesus bids men to come and die."

Saul of Tarsus was crucified positionally in the death of Jesus, but he was also born again personally when Christ came to him on the road to Damascus. This is what is meant when he says, "I have been crucified with Christ." His death saved me.

There is a popular reality show called, "Extreme Make Over." On that show the producers gather experts in cosmetic surgery to give a person a new look—nip this and tuck that, smooth some wrinkles here and add hair there. I am considering applying to get on the show. In the end you have a person who looks practically nothing like the person at the beginning of the show. But of course, the person is the same. Religious works are like that. Through a change of habits and a commitment to a new way of life, you begin to get an extreme make over. You used to smoke; now you don't. You used to lie around in bed and read the New York Times on Sunday morning, eat croissants and imported preserves. But now you are up on Sunday morning, you put on your Sunday face, you force yourself out to go to early church, carry a big Bible and smile a lot. But that is not what Paul is talking about. That is what the false teachers wanted. Observe the law and you will get rid of sin. Paul says, No. You must die. You must recognize your sin and obediently follow Jesus Christ all the way to the cross. In His death on the cross, you are free. The old person is dead.

My beloved, this is altogether a work of the Spirit. Thus, I am confident that an invitation to die to yourself, to repent and see your only hope in the sacrificial

---

[8] John Owens, *The Death of Death in the Death of Christ: A Treatise of the Redemption and Reconciliation That Is in the Blood of Christ, with the Merit Thereof, and Satisfaction Wrought Thereby* (1647). An online version may found at:
http://www.graciouscall.org/books/owen/death/toc.html.

death of Christ is a powerful invitation. For this is the will of God for you. To die that you may be born again.

His Life Empowers Me.

>...It is no longer I who live, but Christ who lives in me... (Galatians 2:20).

Paul, having admitted that he is no longer the same man, also admits that he is not under his own control. It is Christ who is alive in Paul, leading him and guiding him. This man is under another power.

We now move from considering the doctrine of justification to considering the doctrine of union with Christ. This is a beautiful doctrine of the Bible that says that when we are justified, declared holy before God based solely on our faith in the cross of Christ (by faith we mean a transfer of trust from self to total reliance on the merits of Jesus and in obedience to His gospel), we are united to Jesus Christ. He lives in us.

Our union in Christ was taught by Jesus:

> "...I am in my Father, and you are in me, and I am in you" (John 14:20, NIV).

> "I am the vine; you are the branches. If a man remains in me and I in him, he will bear much fruit; apart from me you can do nothing." (John 15:5, NIV).

> "...I pray...that all of them may be one, Father, just as you are in me and I am in you. May they also be in us so that the world may believe that you have sent me" (John 17:20, 21, NIV).

Paul taught and told the Corinthians,

> ...You are not your own; you were bought at a price... (1 Corinthians 6:19, 20, NIV).

It was interesting having Pastor Bob here last week. A number of you told me how you have seen his ministry in me. I assure you that we are different in many ways, but I am certain your observations are true. There is a sense in which his many years of teaching me, of guiding me, of telling me really corny jokes have influenced me!

The life of my wife has empowered me. I am different because we have walked together these many years. This week I told someone that being your pastor for the last two and a half years has been a life-transforming experience for me. I am not the same man I was when I came here. I do not mean it to be self-congratulatory when I say, I am better. I mean to say that your lives, your dreams, your passions, your responses to sorrow have molded me. I cannot imagine preaching without that power flowing through me.

In an infinitely more supernatural and transforming way, I can no longer imagine living without the power of Jesus Christ flowing through me. The life of our Lord possess those who are His. When His death saves us, we cease to live; but through His life, we truly begin to live again. He comes into our lives and takes control and empowers us in every area of our existence: our relationships, our attitudes, our decisions, our responses to sorrows, our understanding of tragedy, and even our awareness of joy in the midst of it all.

Is Christ alive in you?

His Love Compels Me.
...And the life I now live in the flesh I live by faith in the Son of God, who loved me and gave himself for me (Galatians 2:20).

This last article of Paul's declaration of independence catches us off guard. In the midst of a theological reflection on his struggles for justification by faith, in his talk so filled with the doctrine of union in Christ, the giant theologian caps off his freedom speech with this tender statement: He loved me.

What religion could not do, love did. What a life of hard training in rigorous legal and religious devotion could not do, the love of Christ did.

And this is enormously important to us. When we speak of doctrine, for example justification by faith, we are not toying with language. We are not tickling our intellectual fancy. We are not exercising our theological muscles. We are dealing in love. This is the love of God who gave His only begotten Son.

This story has been told a thousand times, but it bears repeating. When Dr. Karl Barth, arguably the most influential theological figure of the twentieth century, came to the United States in 1961, he gave a lecture at Princeton Seminary. Afterwards Barth took questions. A reporter from the New York Times asked the eminent theologian, "Dr. Barth, can you tell us the theological concept that has had the most profound influence on your thinking?" And the man who wrote a "closely reasoned" systematic theology that took up over 10,000 pages[9] replied:

---
[9] See the web page on the Center for Barth Studies at http://www.ptsem.edu/grow/barth/.

CHAPTER 3   THE TRUE BELIEVER'S DECLARATION OF INDEPENDENCE

> Jesus loves me this I know,
> For the Bible tells me so.

You know in your heart of hearts, that is what you want. You know that most of all you want to be loved. In Jesus of Nazareth the question of God's love is answered in an unequivocal, Yes! When you know that love, when you know that Lord of love, you will never be the same. What turning over a new leaf could not do, what trying really hard to be good could not do, the love of Jesus does without any effort at all.

CONCLUSION

The summary of this declaration and of the whole argument is found in Galatians 2:21:

> I do not nullify the grace of God, for if justification were through the law, then Christ died to no purpose (Galatians 2:21).

I like to call this summary, I will not go back. The question is settled once and for all. God is pleased only with His Son; and if I am in His Son, I am free. For in Christ—and this is our Declaration of Independence—

- His death saves me.
- His life empowers me.
- His love compels me.

The Declaration of Independence created a free people. And I have seen how the true believer's declaration of independence, how trusting in Christ alone, can create free human beings.

I sat with a woman who was still groggy from the anesthesia. The results of her operation were not all that everyone had been praying for. There was a road of treatment ahead that would be challenging. But as we talked, I heard her speak of how she wanted to be a part of our English as a Second Language ministry, which was about to begin. She said, "Just think, a church could be planted right here to reach out to Hispanic people who don't know Jesus." However weak her voice, she talked with an enthusiasm that transformed a sterile hospital room into a sanctuary of the living God. I prayed with her and walked away. But by the time I got to the elevator, I was fighting to hold back tears—tears that came from standing in awe of a faith that was out of this world. It seemed that no disease could destroy her, no circumstance could deny her, not even death would diminish her.

I felt that I might have been in the presence of an angel. Then, about time the elevator opened, I got my theology straight. This was no angel. This was a woman—a woman free from guilt, free from fear. This was a woman who had already died years ago and who was now alive with a power not her own, a power that had brought her peace that this world could never give, a power that brought her a life that will never end, and a power that is available to anyone here.

In Jesus Christ the Year of Jubilee is here. Through His grace all of us may declare, I have been crucified with Christ and it is not longer I who live but Christ who lives in me...

CHAPTER 3   THE TRUE BELIEVER'S DECLARATION OF INDEPENDENCE

Questions for Reflection

1. How does Christian doctrine in Galatians relate to political freedom? What are the differences?

2. In what ways does the atonement of Jesus Christ lead us to freedom and joy?

3. Why is it said, Justification is the defining doctrine of Christianity?

4. What does it mean to "come and die" when we follow Jesus Christ? How did that work out in your own life?

5. How did you have your "Declaration of Independence" in Jesus Christ in your life?

Prayer

O Father of freedom, whose love sent forth Jesus Christ to purchase us from the auction block of sin, work within me a new freedom from every sin that seeks to entangle me, from every pain that seeks to debilitate me, from every faithless moment that seeks to keep me from You, and from every act of boasting in my own supposed powers. Lead me to declare my independence from sin and self by transferring my trust from myself to You. In Jesus' Name.

Amen.

"You are no longer foreigners and aliens, but fellow citizens with God's people and members of God's household."

Ephesians 2:1

"Belonging to the seed of Abraham is not determined by physical descent but by faith."

Hermann Ribberdos

4

WHO IS THE FAMILY OF GOD?

Galatians 3:8-9, 16, 26-29

Who is the family of God? Who are the true sons and daughters of Abraham? That question has provoked responses that have brought about bitterness, hatred, and even bloodshed. Palestinian and Jew, Irish Protestant and Irish Catholic, Arabs and Anglo-America. Is there any hope of peace?

> And the Scripture, foreseeing that God would justify the Gentiles by faith, preached the gospel beforehand to Abraham, saying, "In you shall all the nations be blessed." So then, those who are of faith are blessed along with Abraham, the man of faith (Galatians 3:8-9).
>
> Now the promises were made to Abraham and to his offspring. It does not say, "And to offsprings," referring to many, but referring to one, "And to your offspring," who is Christ (Galatians 3:16).
>
> For in Christ Jesus you are all sons of God, through faith. For as many of you as were baptized into Christ have put on Christ. There is neither Jew nor Greek, there is neither slave nor free, there is neither male nor female, for you are all one in Christ Jesus. And if you are Christ's, then you are Abraham's offspring, heirs according to promise (Galatians 3:26-29).

FAMILY FEUD

There was once a television game show called "Family Feud" where the host went around kissing all the women contestants and one family went up against another family to see who would win. In real life, many family feuds happen, not *between* the Hatfields and the McCoys, but *within* the Hatfields or *within* the McCoys. And there is no game show host going around kissing anyone. And no one wins.

The family feud contest for my friend Allen started out at, of all places, a funeral. Allen had only recently married into the family when his father-in-law died; and they went back to the ancestral home to help make arrangements, attend the funeral, and provide love and care for his mother-in-law. So far this sounds simple. But my friend's sister-in-law hated him and hadn't talked to her sister for many years. Add to that a misunderstanding about who should step in to make arrangements with the funeral home, and you've got yourself a family feud and a week of tension and strife and even painful encounters. Sometimes the things that are supposed to bring healing end up exposing deep-seated bitterness, resentment, and jealousy. The message that came through to my friend was, Why are you even here? You are not family! My friend, who is on active duty in the Army, felt like he just wanted to get back to the war on terrorism so he could get some peace!

Who is in and who is out of a family and how you gain acceptance in a family is real sticky business. One writer on the subject of family feuds within denominations wrote a book with the depressingly real-life title *Reflections on the Roots of Presbyterian Conflict* in which he said,

> Family fights are never simple. Personalities, power-relationships, old wounds and inequities, feelings about the in-laws, concern about status and pedigree, to name but a few, all impinge on family feuds. This is no different in the church.[1]

The Book of Galatians is about a family conflict in the church. Early on, the issue became, Who are the real sons and daughters of Abraham, and how do you get to be one? Though it had always been God's plan for all the families of the earth to come into the family of faith through Abraham, human pride and exclusivism had produced a Jewish nation that excluded others and looked down upon the nations of the earth. God dealt with this when He sent Jonah to Nineveh and showed how even the enemy of Israel could be brought to faith. Isaiah reminded Israel that "it is too small a thing" that the coming Messiah would be only for the tribe of Jacob.[2] He would be a light to the world. And in Jesus Christ, this plan of God to build a people—not through a bloodline but through faith—came to glorious fruition. Jesus scolded those who thought that they were true Israel but who denied Him. He told them that they were not of Abraham but of their father the devil.[3] Hard words. Indeed, in the book of Revelation Jesus writes to His people in Asia Minor who are being persecuted by unbelieving Judaizers. He says that they are not Jews but are the synagogue

---

[1] Bradley J. Longfield, *Reflections on the Roots of Presbyterian Conflict: A Background Paper for the Atlanta Conference, Spring 1999,* University of Dubuque Theological Seminary (http://horeb.pcusa.org/oga/diversity/appendices.htm).
[2] Isaiah 49:6.
[3] John 8:42, 44

of Satan.[4] And in Romans 11, Paul warned Gentile believers who had been engrafted into true Israel not to forget that the gospel came to the Jews first and then to the Greeks.[5] All over the place there seemed to be family feuds.

Today, of course, we have it all settled, right? Our churches are filled with people of all races, all backgrounds with no prejudice, no racial strife, no question about who is in and who is out. Right?

As Dr. John Perkins reminded us, race and class problems still plague the church of Jesus Christ today. So the question is as relevant now as it was in first century Galatia. Who are God's people? Who are the sons and daughters of Abraham? In Galatians 3, the Lord wants us to know two key truths about the people of God. As you will see, these two truths have a great bearing on our Communion this morning.

God's People Are Saved through One Faith

For as many of you as were baptized into Christ have put on Christ (Galatians 3:27).

This is a very important piece of the debate in Galatians. Formerly, circumcision was the sign of entrance into the people of God. If you were a foreigner and wanted to be part of Israel, the male head of the family would represent his whole household and be circumcised. But now Paul says that coming into the family of God is through baptism into Christ, putting on Christ.

There are some things that Paul is not saying and some things that he is saying.

He is not saying that the sign of water baptism saves. Listen to John Stott on this passage:

> We must give Paul credit for a consistent theology. This whole Epistle is devoted to the theme that we are justified through faith, not circumcision. It is inconceivable that Paul should now substitute baptism for circumcision and teach that they are [saved] in Christ by baptism! The apostle clearly makes *faith* the means of our union with Christ.[6]

He is saying that the act of baptism signifies what faith is accomplishing through Jesus Christ. In this way baptism replaces circumcision. The truth is, of course,

---

[4] Revelation 2:9
[5] Romans 11:17, 18
[6] John Stott, *The Message of Galatians* (Leicester, England: Inter-Varsity Press, 1968), 99.

that circumcision could not save. Signs are important, but they point to a deeper spiritual reality.

Paul is saying that we become a child of God when we are engrafted into the tree, when we are anointed by the Spirit in Christ. There is no other way. Faith is what every person in God's family has in common. And when speaking of faith, there is only one faith. It is popular today to speak of faith in a sort of ecumenical, nondescript way. We hear about "people of faith" and "faith-based" programs. But let us be clear that this is not what the Bible is speaking of. The faith that unites all of God's true believers is not a man-centered faith, but a faith in the one Savior, our Lord Jesus Christ, supernaturally wrought in the soul by the Holy Spirit. Only when we have that faith, are we united in Him.

Paul put it this way in Ephesians:

> There is one body and one Spirit—just as you were called to the one hope that belongs to your call—one Lord, one faith, one baptism, one God and Father of all, who is over all and through all and in all (Ephesians 4:4-6).

In Galatians (and particularly here in Galatians 3) there is only one faith. How was Abraham saved? The same way Paul was saved and the same way the Galatians were saved—by faith in God's Redeemer who has baptized us into Christ.

I mentioned a funeral where a family had a feud, but someone else told me about how they found healing at a funeral. Where there were old wounds, through their common bond in the love of their loved one, there was the oil of healing of relationships. Where there were old resentments, through their common suffering, there was new restoration. Where there was estrangement, through their common memory, the estrangement became an embrace. And at the center of it all was the body of their loved one—in death bringing them all together.

The death of Jesus on the cross is how we come together. And at the center of our lives is the body of the One who loved us. That is what Communion really is all about—all of us from different backgrounds, different dreams, being brought together around the body and blood of our Loved One.

God's people are simply those saved by one faith—faith in the finished work of Jesus Christ on the cross. Nothing more. Nothing less.

God's People Are Saved into One Family

> There is no longer Jew or Greek, there is no longer slave or free, there is no longer male and female; for all of you are one in Christ Jesus. And if you belong to Christ, then you are Abraham's offspring, heirs according to the promise (Galatians 3:28, 29, NRSV).

Paul could not make it any clearer.

Paul would write in Ephesians,

> For he himself is our peace, who has made the two one and has destroyed the barrier, the dividing wall of hostility, (Ephesians 2:14, NIV).

In Christ, there is one family.

It is popular to speak of the family of man, the family of humanity, and so forth. This is true. We are one people since we all bear the image of God. But also we all bear the mark of the fall, the marring of that sacred image, which has to be healed. And only those who have faith in Christ Jesus as their living Lord and Savior are brought back into a family relationship with the Father.

This one family in Christ brings genuine organic unity among all peoples, and here Paul shows how Christ obliterates any distinctive that would divide the way people come to Christ and become children of God in Christ.

Christ has torn down racism

> There is no longer Jew or Greek… (Galatians 3:28, NRSV).

The issue in Galatia again deals with Jewish prejudice against Gentiles. The sons and daughters of Abraham were by faith. Now this doesn't mean that the Jew had no special place in the economy of God's work. Paul will say in Romans that the gospel is the power of God unto salvation to the Jew first and then to the Gentile.[7] God's covenant of grace was promised through the man of faith. God promised a nation and under Moses, a nation arose. God promised a land, and under Joshua a land was secured. From those people came a Messiah, the Lord Jesus Christ. But this covenant of grace administered under the old covenant was always intended to blossom forth to the whole world. For "it was too small a thing" for the gospel to be only for the Jew. But it most certainly began there.

Racism can go both ways, as history has tragically shown us. I want to return to something I alluded to earlier in Romans 11. The same Paul who wrote

---
[7] Romans 1:16

Galatians and who taught that the sons of Abraham included all who by faith in Jesus came into the family of God, also taught in Romans that the Gentiles must beware of racism or pride

> But if some of the branches were broken off, and you, although a wild olive shoot, were grafted in among the others and now share in the nourishing root of the olive tree, do not be arrogant toward the branches. If you are, remember it is not you who support the root, but the root that supports you (Romans 11:17).

Pride and hate and bitterness are the seeds of racism that produce enmity and strife. We need to remember that we are called into one family. When they put on Christ, Africans, Europeans, Jews, Arabs, Asians, Hispanics are all a part of the one true family of God. We need to remember the little children's song and not only sing it, but reflect it in our lives and our relations to others:

> Jesus loves the little children,
> All the children of the world.
> Red and yellow, black and white,
> All are precious in His sight,
> Jesus loves the little children of the world.

Christ has also torn down sexism
> ...there is no longer male or female... (Galatians 3:28, NRSV).

The radical feminist agenda would do well to remember that before Jesus Christ, women were relegated to second-class citizens. The effect of the fall created a hostility between men and women that, without Christ, threatened our being able to live out our very humanity in peace. In fact, at the time of Paul, even Jewish rabbis might be heard to remark, "Thank God, that I was not born a Gentile or a woman." This was wrong. In Jesus Christ women are redeemed and truly liberated from such oppression. Womankind was infused with nobility in Christ. It was a woman who brought forward Christ. It was women who cared for the needs of our Savior, and who can ever forget the women who poured incense on His feet? Who can remember how Jesus forgave the adulteress, or healed the woman who reached out to touch the hem of His garment? When all had abandoned our Lord, save the beloved John, women stood at the foot of the cross to comfort Jesus with their presence and their love. The first human beings to see Jesus alive were women.

This does not erase the role relationships in the body of Christ. Paul will clearly teach that he will not allow a woman to exercise spiritual authority over a man in the church. And it does not blur the role relationships of women and men in marriage, given by the Holy Spirit in Ephesians 5 and in 1 Peter 3. But without any doubt, it tears down the hatred and enmity that exists between men and women. In Christ the reprehensible attitudes and conduct toward women is replaced with what they would have never known: chivalry, nobility, and the cherishing of women. And it called for women to lovingly esteem and honor men.

Christ also tore down the wall of classism
...there is no longer slave or free... (Galatians 3:27, NRSV).

This was an amazing statement because the ancient world, like much of the world today, was divided into castes, classes, sets and subsets of human beings based on lineage, education, national status, or even physical ability. But Paul explodes this. Yes, there are still superiors and inferiors in work and in many other areas of life. Paul's words are not an endorsement for an unrestrained egalitarianism where no one is subject to anyone else. Comparing Scripture to Scripture clears that up. Paul is declaring that in Jesus Christ we are all equal before the cross. No one human being has any greater worth than another and in Jesus Christ that truth is fully realized. The whole of the Bible deals with rich and poor relations. All of the Old Testament commands find their meaning in Christ. All of the New Testament examples of conflict over class find their answers in the centrality of Jesus Christ.

The apostle who wrote this book about freedom in Christ, practices what he preaches about classism in one of my favorite books of the Bible, Philemon. In that little twenty-five-verse letter tucked in between Titus and Hebrews, we see how Paul, through the centrality of Christ, brought together a family. A slave named Onesimus had apparently escaped from Philemon, a wealthy man who was a Christian. The text says, at least, that this slave might have "wronged" his master[8] by being in Rome rather than with Philemon. But Onesimus, the slave, was converted to Christ under Paul's ministry. What is appealing and alarming about this letter is that three times Paul calls himself a prisoner or a man in chains.[9] So in writing about a slave, Paul, who could have used apostolic authority, appeals to Philemon by identifying himself with the slave. Indeed, he says that Onesimus is his "child," his son[10], and his "very heart."[11] Paul and Onesimus the slave are family. And he calls Philemon his brother[12] and Apphia, perhaps Philemon's wife, is Paul's "sister."[13] He then tells

---
[8] Philemon 18
[9] Philemon 1, 10, 23
[10] Philemon 10
[11] Philemon 12
[12] Philemon 7, 20
[13] Philemon 2

the master that, because Onesimus has come to faith in Christ, Philemon should now welcome back this man "no longer as a slave but more than a slave, as a beloved brother."[14] Paul then seals his letter with these words, "the grace of the Lord Jesus Christ be with your spirit." Once that grace which saved Philemon is stirred up through the Holy Spirit, he will see that Paul and Onesimus and Philemon are all slaves—slaves to grace and love. And they are also all brothers, family through Jesus Christ. We are saved into one family.

Recently I went to an Army promotion ceremony involving a young African-American captain who was being promoted to major. His wife was there, and his two beautiful little girls stole the show as they wiggled and grinned and thoroughly enjoyed the spotlight while their mamma pinned the new rank on their daddy. Then the new major spoke a few words. He thanked his wife, his parents, and spoke of his love for his brothers and sisters in uniform who had become family to him. That was emotional enough in itself. But then he surprised us all. As he looked down from the platform at a young captain, a white man, the black major teared up. "And I want to thank the godfather to my children." The two men had shared so much common life together in the Army that when the black major's children were born, he had asked his white friend to be there to raise his children if anything ever happened to him and his wife. Through their common commitment, they became brothers.

Through our common commitment to Jesus Christ, we are brothers and sisters in Him.

Conclusion

So the answer to the question, Who are the sons and daughters of Abraham? leads to the Biblical conviction, Through Jesus Christ we are saved by one faith and saved into one family. The family of God is comprised of those who have put on Christ. And when we embrace the love and forgiveness of Jesus Christ, something wonderful happens.

What happens is family.

Thomas Tarrants III was a white supremacist. Thomas Tarrants III believed that America was a nation for Anglo-Saxons only, and he hated Jews and Africans, among others. He hated them so much that he led paramilitaristic efforts to get ready for war against other races. One day this activity led him into a gun battle with law enforcement authorities in Mississippi. He was sent to prison.

---

[14] Philemon 16

Another man was John Perkins, a black man that we heard this past week. You who were here heard him tell how he was the son of a sharecropper and how his brother was murdered by a white law enforcement officer. John Perkins went to a different kind of prison—a prison of pain and hatred.

But the two men became sons of God when the grace of Jesus Christ overwhelmed their lives. Forgiven and free, they went in search of reconciliation, and God brought them together. Now John Perkins and Thomas Tarrants tell the story of how God brought them together and how, through Jesus Christ, they became family. The title of their book tells it all: *He's My Brother.*

What if we could see a world where white Klansmen and Black Muslims knelt side by side? Or what if Palestinians and Israelis could embrace? What if Irish Protestants and Irish Catholics could walk hand-in-hand? What if parents and adult children could speak without hurting each other? Or what if some of you picked up the phone and called an estranged loved one to say, I love you, or an estranged friend to say, I miss you. Or what if you could call the lawyers, tear up the papers, and say, I am sorry, honey; I want to come back home.

The Communion Table testifies, now and always, that "What if" has become "It is finished."

Hope and healing and becoming one as a family are not only possible, but are inevitable when you come to Jesus Christ by faith.

God invites you to come into His family.

Questions for Reflection

1. What family feuds were going on in the early church in Galatia? How could genuine believers exasperate these feuds? How do we stop them while being faithful to Scripture?

2. If Old Testament saints were saved in the way we are saved, what were the differences?

3. Were those mandating a return to the Old Testament sign of circumcision among those who are the family of God, and what was their motivation?

4. Does ethnicity matter in terms of salvation, and if not, how is it that Gentiles who believe are the children of Abraham and some ethnic Hebrews are not?

5. What do we mean when we speak of the "oneness and unity of the people of God" in all of the Bible?

6. What is the responsibility of Christians today to those who seek division in the body of Christ?

7. How can believers promote Christ-like harmony without being paternalistic?

Prayer

O Father of all, who has revealed that You are not just Father-Creator but Abba-Father to those who come to You through Your Son Jesus, shatter my prejudices, self-righteous attitudes, and smugness in the face of so many needs and so great a salvation. In Jesus' name.

Amen.

> "In the law...God is seen as the rewarder of perfect righteousness and the avenger of sin. But in Christ, His face shines out, full of grace and gentleness to poor, unworthy sinners."
>
> John Calvin

> "The utility of the law is that it convinces man of his weakness, and compels him to apply for the medicine of grace, which is in Christ."
>
> Augustine

5

BORN FREE

Galatians 4:21-31

We come now to the closing argument of Paul's defense of the gospel of grace. After this closing illustration and restatement of his proposition, Paul will move on to apply the gospel of grace in godly living.

Everyone knows that closing illustrations are meant to tie up the whole message, and this is what Paul does. Having dealt with Abraham and shown that all who believe in Christ Jesus are the children of Abraham, having established that salvation is only by the grace of God through faith, Paul employs an Old Testament story to make his point.

> Tell me, you who desire to be under the law, do you not listen to the law? For it is written that Abraham had two sons, one by a slave woman and one by a free woman. But the son of the slave was born according to the flesh, while the son of the free woman was born through promise. Now this may be interpreted allegorically: these women are two covenants. One is from Mount Sinai, bearing children for slavery; she is Hagar. Now Hagar is Mount Sinai in Arabia; she corresponds to the present Jerusalem, for she is in slavery with her children. But the Jerusalem above is free, and she is our mother. For it is written,
>
> "Rejoice, O barren one who does not bear;
> break forth and cry aloud, you who are not in labor!
> For the children of the desolate one will be more
> than those of the one who has a husband."
>
> Now you, brothers, like Isaac, are children of promise. But just as at that time he who was born according to the flesh persecuted him who was born according to the Spirit, so also it is now. But what does the Scripture say? "Cast out the slave woman and her son, for the son of the slave woman shall not inherit with the son of the free woman." So,

brothers, we are not children of the slave but of the free woman. (Galatians 4:21-31)

HOW LITTLE ELIAN LOST HIS LIBERTY

On Thanksgiving Day, 1999, a woman, trying to escape from a dictatorship in Cuba, realized that the wind and waves and weather of the Florida straits were going to kill her. She put her little boy, Elian, on an inner tube and said a prayer for him to be guided to the shores of America and find freedom. The six-year-old child claimed that dolphins guided his inner tube to safety on America's shores. Others thought those dolphins may have had some help. But little Elian Gonzales from Cuba became the center of a national debate in America: should he stay in the country his mother died trying to get to or should he be returned to the land she sought to escape from. An international custody battle ensued between his biological father back in Cuba and his relatives in Florida. No matter what you thought should have been done about the custody situation, who could ever forget the gripping television images of federal agents breaking into a home and taking Elian by force, whisking him away to be returned to the dictatorship of Fidel Castro.

Little Elian was born into slavery to a tyrant, but for one moment, it seemed, he breathed freedom. But he returned to the slavery of Communist Cuba.

We who witnessed it felt something. Maybe we felt pain over the fear in the eyes of that child as U.S. Federal agents forcibly removed him. But I think most of us felt the horror of having once tasted freedom, losing it.

HOW A FAITHFUL FOLLOWER LOST HER FREEDOM

This week I talked to a woman from another town and another church who told me that she had been born again as a child, having heard the gospel. She once had thought of her faith as a source of freedom, but it soon became a prison. Misguided by one teacher after another, this poor Christian woman was led into a circle that grew smaller and smaller. Increasingly and imperceptibly, like a frog in a kettle being slowly heated to a boil, she was trapped. Her beliefs became so narrow and so rigid, her view of other people conditioned by one litmus test after another, until she finally found that she could not associate with any other Christian unless they, too, lived within the confines of her theological and experiential circle. She even began to suspect other Christians' profession of faith unless they lived in her circle. She found that she could no longer associate with old friends who had not followed her into her circle. Instead of a heart that longed for others to come to Christ, she longed for the circle to draw tighter. In this mindset, her own supposed orthodoxy was confirming her growing isolation. But one day it became too much, and she began to cry. The circle was completely drawn in, and no one was in her small circle but herself. She had tasted the joy of Christ, but now it had been taken from her, and she was in slavery again.

I have seen this happen in many ways in the lives of Christians. When we leave the central teaching of the gospel—we are sinners saved only by the gracious love of God in Christ—and we make anything else a condition to faith, we are little Elians in the arms of a dark and sinister force bringing us back into bondage. When we leave the way of the cross and begin to think that life can be lived without Christ, we also begin the slide into slavery. When we think of the gospel plus something else, we draw circles around our lives and are cut off from the life-giving power and joy and freedom that Jesus brings.

How God Used an "Apostle of the Heart Set Free" to Rescue Christians on Their Way to Slavery

Like Elian, Paul sees his saints at Galatia being whisked away by false teachers who are taking the them back into the bondage of salvation by the law. Like the woman I met, the Galatians were withdrawing from freedom into a smaller and smaller circle. They were like the frogs in the kettle and had no idea the water was getting hotter.

So Paul used an Old Testament account as a decisive final illustration to loosen the encroaching chains of religion and bring true believers back to authentic Christianity.

Paul reminds me, not of a SWAT team, but of a Navy SEAL breaking into the camp of terrorists to release hostages. And what he says is like three clicks, three turns of the key that unlocks the chains and releases the hostages.

There are three turns of the key that we need to remember in order to keep our freedom as followers of Christ.

The first turn of the key to freedom is

True Believers Are Born Free

> Tell me, you who desire to be under the law, do you not listen to the law? For it is written that Abraham had two sons, one by a slave woman and one by a free woman. But the son of the slave was born according to the flesh, while the son of the free woman was born

> through promise. Now this may be interpreted allegorically: these women are two covenants. One is from Mount Sinai, bearing children for slavery; she is Hagar. Now Hagar is Mount Sinai in Arabia; she corresponds to the present Jerusalem, for she is in slavery with her children. (Galatians 4:21-25)

A Christo-centric Story

Before we get into the story, we need to see what Paul is doing. Paul uses a story from the Old Testament that would have been very well known by the false teachers and also by the Galatian Christians who would have heard this story from the false teachers. By his own admission in Galatians 4:24, Paul is interpreting the Old Testament as an allegory showing those who are free in Christ and those who are fast bound in bondage to religion.

An allegory is a literary devise that uses parts of a story to be symbolic for meanings not indicated on the surface. Generally this can be dangerous. Rather than taking the truth from the passage, there is the temptation to bring ones own interpretation into the passage and the parts of the story become a prop for that interpretation. But Paul is not just anyone. His words are inspired. Moreover, he is showing, as almost all commentators agree, that this very part of redemptive history is loaded with meaning. While Paul uses the word allegory, he is really showing how the people and places are types for grace and legalism.

In all of this we need to see that Paul, writing the very Word of God, shows how the Old Testament stories were all Christ centric. Everything written in the Old must be interpreted by the New. Everything in the New is blossoming forth out of the Old. One immediately thinks of the life's work of Dr. Edmund Clowney[1] of Westminster Seminary whose books *Preaching Christ in All of Scripture* and *The Unfolding Mystery: Discovering Christ in the Old Testament* remind us that the entire Bible is about Jesus. The critic would say that when you do that, you are not faithful to the immediate text, which is not about Jesus but about Adam or about Abraham or about Moses or about some historical event. But we would say, Look at how Paul handles all of redemptive history and is able to draw it all together in the gospel. Look at Jesus Himself in Luke 24:27:

> And beginning with Moses and all the Prophets, he interpreted to them in all the Scriptures the things concerning himself (Luke 24:27).

---

[1] Edmund P. Clowney, *Preaching Christ in All of Scripture* (Wheaton, IL: Crossway Books, 2003); *The Unfolding Mystery: Discovering Christ in the Old Testament* (Colorado Springs, CO: NavPress, 1988).

The entire Bible teaches about the gospel of God's grace in Jesus Christ. And so Paul concludes his proposition that the true children of Abraham are those who trust in Jesus Christ by drawing attention to this Old Testament story.

He teaches that there are deeper spiritual truths beneath two sons, two mothers, and two places.

A Story of Two Sons and Two Mothers and Two Places

I will get to the two places in a moment, but the two sons in this text refer to Isaac and Ishmael. Both were sons of Abraham, yet they had two different mothers. Ishmael's mother was an Egyptian maidservant, Hagar; and Isaac's mother was Sarah, Abraham's wife. God had made a covenant with Abraham that from him God would make a nation, give them a land, and from these people and this land God's covenant, bringing salvation, would extend to all of the peoples of the earth. But first there had to be a son. Since Sarah was beyond childbearing years, when this news came, she had a good laugh.[2] Indeed, there was a time in Sarah's life when the promise seemed like a dream that could never come true. So out of doubt, despair, and impatience, two parallel stories began which have repercussions to this day. Sarah's impatience over the promise of the Lord turned to conniving, and she told Abraham to take her maid Hagar, a young woman, and they could have the promised child[3]. This was how Ishmael was born—out of doubt, human reasoning, man-centered plans. For Paul, this was the law—a man-centered theology that does not trust God but leans on its own devices. It is not of God, and as Ishmael was rejected as the one to bring forth the line of the Messiah, so God rejects all human religions that do not trust in His plan of salvation. On the other hand, there was Isaac. His name means laughter. God had the last laugh, we might say. This child, born to the aged couple, would be the one through whom God would raise up His Son, Jesus Christ, to fulfill the ancient promise to bless the world. For Paul, this was the gospel of grace, the plan of salvation. Isaac, laughter and joy, was born from above, a true miracle baby, and so true faith comes from above.

This is what John says,

> Yet to all who received him, to those who believed in his name, he gave the right to become children of God—children born not of natural descent, nor of human decision or a husband's will, but born of God (John 1:12,13, NIV).

---

[2] Genesis 18:12
[3] Genesis 16:1-3

Paul's closing illustration is central to authentic Christianity. True believers are born
- Free of human power
- Free of human reasoning
- Free of man-centered ideas
- And thus free—from God above, by grace alone, through faith alone, in Christ alone, and to the glory of God alone

And this freedom begets freedom.

In the Gospel of John a controversy broke out between Jesus and the Pharisees over the very same matter afflicting the Galatian church.

> "and you will know the truth, and the truth will set you free." They answered him, "We are offspring of Abraham and have never been enslaved to anyone. How is it that you say, 'You will become free'?" (John 8:32-33).

They did not see that true freedom comes not from bloodline or from religious ritual but only from above. Thus Jesus said,

> "So if the Son sets you free, you will be free indeed" (John 8:36).

I pray that you know that freedom. It is a freedom that comes from being born again by the Spirit of God. I pray that you will come today and lay hold of that freedom. As dolphins guided Elian, so the Spirit of God will guide you. What you want most in your heart is here. Your soul is longing for freedom. And that freedom is Jesus Christ. Once you find that freedom, my beloved, Jesus says to you,

> "My Father, who has given them to me, is greater than all, and no one is able to snatch them out of the Father's hand" (John 10:29).

Jesus is saying that no SWAT team from hell will ever be able to snatch you out of His arms.

That leads us to the second turn of the key that loosens us from the chains of oppressiveness.

True Believers Must Live Free

> Now Hagar is Mount Sinai in Arabia; she corresponds to the present Jerusalem, for she is in slavery with her children. But the Jerusalem above is free, and she is our mother. For it is written,
> "Rejoice, O barren one who does not bear;
> break forth and cry aloud, you who are not in labor!

> For the children of the desolate one will be more
> than those of the one who has a husband" (Galatians 4:25-27).

We have discussed the two sons and the two mothers, but there are also two places in this story.

A Place Called Freedom

Stories are made up not only of people but of places. In the Old Testament, the story of how God gave Israel the law came through a mountain. Mount Sinai was the place where God gave the law to Moses. Paul equates that with an understanding that salvation comes by law. Of course, it never did, but such a mistaken understanding had arisen among God's people and that was the idea that Paul was battling in Galatia. So Paul uses their own sign of the law, Mount Sinai, and adds, not for geographical specificity but for theological emphasis, that such a Mount is in Arabia. In other words, this is not really in Israel. Yet, Paul says this is what is corresponding to Jerusalem today. This is an unbelievably provocative statement. He is saying that present teaching coming from those who would restrict God's grace in Christ and add anything to it is not true Israel. Then Paul adds that the true Jerusalem is not even there but is "above and free and she is our mother."

In the New Testament, the Jerusalem that was the capitol of the physical people of the Old Covenant yields to the New Jerusalem, which is a spiritual and eternal place in heaven. Thus, twice in Revelation we read about the new Jerusalem coming down out of heaven from God.[4]

We also read about how the Old Testament physical has now been powerfully updated in the New Testament spiritual:

> For you have not come to what may be touched, a blazing fire and darkness and gloom and a tempest and the sound of a trumpet and a voice whose words made the hearers beg that no further messages be spoken to them. For they could not endure the order that was given, "If even a beast touches the mountain, it shall be stoned." Indeed, so terrifying was the sight that Moses said, "I tremble with fear." But you have come to Mount Zion and to the city of the living God, the heavenly Jerusalem, and to innumerable angels in festal gathering, and to the assembly of the firstborn who are enrolled in heaven, and to God, the judge of all, and to the spirits of the righteous made perfect, and to Jesus, the mediator of a new covenant, and to the sprinkled blood that speaks a better word than the blood of Abel (Hebrews 12:18-24).

---

[4] Revelation 3:12; 21:2

Freedom Is Locating Home

Craig Barnes. in his book *Searching for Home,* sums up well what Paul is saying to these groups.

> "From its beginning the church has always thought about home more in terms of community than in land or stationary temples...Home is the place where we were created to live from eternity and for eternity—with our true family of Father, Son and Holy Spirit."[5]

Paul is saying that we are free when we focus on our home, heaven, not on anything that is physical and of this world.

According to the U.S. Census Bureau about 43 million Americans will move this year.[6] Most of them move to get a better job. And there is nothing wrong with that. Our country was founded, at least in part, by people wanting a better life. But as a pastor I have found that some job transfers happen in the context of an endless search for finding home, for finding some tangible thing—money, house, position, prestige—that will give meaning to life. They are searching for a home.

Paul is saying that the Old Testament places had a purpose. Temples and buildings and mountains and places on this earth may help in pointing us to God, but they cannot add anything to the security of home or to our soul's freedom. Our home is with Christ. And where He is, there we are free. Again, the gospel plus nothing else—this is the way we live.

If we are born free and ought to live free, there is one final turn of the key.

True Believers Ought to Remain Free

> But what does the Scripture say? "Cast out the slave woman and her son, for the son of the slave woman shall not inherit with the son of the free woman." So, brothers, we are not children of the slave but of the free woman (Galatians 4:30-31).

Paul ends his charge to the Galatians by saying that they must now make the decisive move. The Word has come to them. A free and joyful life awaits them. He is saying that they must not only cast out the false teachers who are drawing them into bondage but they must themselves get out of the shadows and come into the light of God's grace.

---

[5] M. Craig Barnes, *Searching for Home: Spirituality for Restless Soul* (Grand Rapids, MI: Brazos Press, 2003), 33.
[6] Ibid., 15.

As Paul will say later in this book,

> Since we live by the Spirit, let us keep in step with the Spirit (Galatians 5:25, NIV).

If we do not persist in grace, we will surely slip into the bondage of legalism. We do that by making something other than the free offer of the gospel the center of our lives. I have heard of fellowships that are formed out of the centrality of common interests like home schooling or classical education or the centrality of political action or the centrality of one particular eschatological position or another or the centrality of spiritual gifts or an identification with a particular historical figure or how we dress or a million other things.

But there is only one central way to remain free: center on Christ crucified, Christ risen, and Christ among us. The only way to stay in the Spirit is to stay in Christ, center on His gospel, focus on the great commission of Jesus Christ, focus on study of the Word of God, concentrate in daily prayer, seek a community here at our church that focuses on welcoming people into a life centered on the cross of Christ. Any deviation from the centrality of the cross of Christ not only compromises the ordinary day-in and day-out work of the gospel in our lives, but leads us onto a wrong path.

Some years ago the Archbishop of Canterbury was rushing to catch a train in London. In his haste, he accidentally jumped on the wrong passenger car and found himself in a car full of inmates from a mental hospital. They were all dressed in mental hospital clothing. Just as the train pulled out of the station, an orderly came in and began to count the inmates, "1-2-3-4...," when suddenly he saw this distinguished looking gentleman wearing a business suit and a clerical collar. He said, "Who are you?" The answer came back, "I am the Archbishop of Canterbury!" The orderly said: "5-6-7-8."

For a Christian or a congregation to focus on anything other than the cross of Christ is to be on a train with a bunch of legalistic lunatics bound for nowhere. It is best to get off and get free and remain free. If you are not on the gospel train, this Scripture is a call to get off at this stop. And remain free.

Conclusion

We are born free. Live free. Remain free. We are like Isaac. Christianity is the "laughing" surprise of God in the face of our folly. Grace is the unrestrained joy of barren people.

A few months ago, I was doing a Bible study with a couple who were preparing for infant baptism. Incidentally, we do this with every couple who presents their child for baptism. In the course of our time together, these proud parents said, "This baby is a miracle baby." They told me about how the little pre-born child faced great physical challenges, but was born. Many people have told me about their miracle babies. Some were told they could never have children, and then God blessed them through adoption or through a surprise announcement. In other cases a child is born and lives in spite of overwhelming physical problems. Or maybe a special needs child comes into a family's life. That child, too, is a sort of miracle baby—a baby that changes everything, yet brings unimaginable joy and hope to a family. That is what we mean by a miracle baby. Do you think those children are special to parents? Do you think that their world now revolves around protecting and nourishing that child? You bet.

Every born-again child of God is a miracle baby. Prayed for. Supernaturally conceived. Divinely delivered. Then, loved of God. Never forgotten. Never forsaken.

And just as Paul fought for these children of God to stay free, I and all pastors are charged to do the same. Preach grace. Center on the cross. And I plead with you, Don't let anything, any hobby horse, any idea, any program, any movement, or anything in this world take that "Isaac"—that laughing grace of God—from you. To prevent it, keep the cross of Jesus Christ at the center, keep His life flowing through you in Word, sacrament, and prayer. Keep close to His heart by always living to help others claim their miracle of grace.

Questions for Reflection

1. In the Scripture passage for this chapter, how is one born free?

2. Apply the allegory of this passage to religions of the world.

3. In what way may a believer or a church begin to repeat the Galatian error? What are the consequences for the Christian life?

4. How does a focus on heaven make a believer free? How does one practically focus on heaven?

5. Remember the miracle of your new birth? What were the events that led you to Christ? Your parents? A friend? Your pastor? You have grown since that time, but how can remembering the story of how God set you free help you to remain free?

Prayer

Lord of true freedom, I too quickly hold out my hands to the ropes and chains of this present world and trade in my supernatural freedom in Christ for the bondage of religion. Free me today, Lord Jesus. Release me from not only the snare of a works-based righteousness, which is no righteousness at all, but also release me from the temptation to trade my God gained liberty for the cheap thrills of this age. In Christ's holy name I pray.

Amen.

"Since we have these promises, beloved, let us cleanse ourselves from every defilement of body and spirit, bringing holiness to completion in the fear of God."

2 Corinthians 7:1

"Believing and doing are blood-friends."

Samuel Rutherford

6

PRACTICAL HOLINESS

Galatians 5:16-26

George Whitefield said,

…that which doth not tend to promote holiness is not of God.[1]

All theology is practical. All knowledge of God leads to a new way of life. Thus, Paul takes a turn in Galatians 5. He moves from a defense of his ministry being from God, a defense of salvation being of grace alone through faith, his proposition that only those who have faith in Jesus are true descendants of Abraham, to how that applies to following God's law and to getting along with others.

> I say, walk by the Spirit, and you will not gratify the desires of the flesh. For the desires of the flesh are against the Spirit, and the desires of the Spirit are against the flesh, for these are opposed to each other, to keep you from doing the things you want to do. But if you are led by the Spirit, you are not under the law. Now the works of the flesh are evident: sexual immorality, impurity, sensuality, idolatry, sorcery, enmity, strife, jealousy, fits of anger, rivalries, dissensions, divisions, envy, drunkenness, orgies, and things like these. I warn you, as I warned you before, that those who do such things will not inherit the kingdom of God. But the fruit of the Spirit is love, joy, peace, patience, kindness, goodness, faithfulness, gentleness, self-control; against such things there is no law. And those who belong to Christ Jesus have crucified the flesh with its passions and desires. If we live by the Spirit, let us also walk by the Spirit. Let us not become conceited, provoking one another, envying one another (Galatians 5:16-26).

---

[1] Mark Water, comp., *The New Encyclopedia of Christian Quotations* (Grand Rapids, MI: Baker Books, 2000), 478.

GALATIAN GRAFFITI

Graffiti is the act of expressing an opinion by writing on someone else's property, generally in a public place. Writing on the walls of other people's property is against the law, and often what is written is not repeatable. Graffiti has been around since the beginning of time. Recently my son and I were in a restroom and used one of the warm air hand dryers. The instructions were written clearly: push button to turn on machine; place hands under dryer; rub hands briskly. To that, someone—obviously agitated—took the time to scribble, Dry hands on pants.

What if we could go back and read Galatian graffiti at the time the book of Galatians was written? We would likely see examples of the intense factionalism that was present there: Judaizers who required circumcision to be saved, Gentiles who gloried in grace but didn't show it to others, and so-called Christians who hijacked grace in order to justify their love of sinning (Gary Stanley wrote a book called *The Garimus File: A Back-Door Look at the New Testament*. In that book the author imagines what the graffiti must have looked like on the walls of first century Galatia. Of course, all of that was just the product of a fertile imagination, but "In context and tone," writes the New Testament scholar Scott McKnight, "these slogans aptly capture the atmosphere at Galatia."[2]).

Someone supporting the Judaizers point of view scribbled in big red letters, "A promise is a promise!" referring to the law. But a disciple of Paul's wrote, "Abraham was a Gentile." At another place on the wall someone wrote, "Long live the law!" To which a Christian scratched out, "Long live the law" and wrote, "Long live life!" Someone else wrote beside that, "Life stinks!" And then someone else wrote, "Grace isn't cheap but it is free." Someone else, a Judaizer, wrote, "Nothing is free." Then an aspiring poet scribbled out his poem:

> There was a young man named Saul
> Who changed his first name to Paul
>   It didn't make him an apostle
>   or anything colossal,
> Just a fellow with an awful lot of gall.

It was bitter. What started out as a theological argument had racial overtones, sociological implications, and likely even political implications. Wrong assumptions were being made by one side; spurious accusations were being made by the other side. And in all of it, the person of Jesus was not to be found. In

---

[2] Gary Stanley, *The Garimus File: A Back-Door Look at the New Testament* (Sam Bernardino, CA: Here's Life Publishers, 1983) cited by Scott McKnight, *The NIV Application Commentary: Galatians* (Grand Rapids: Zondervan, 1995), 275-276.

fact, this sounds like what is going on in most church quarrels today! In this bitter context Paul dealt with Judaizers, but he also dealt with those who were saying, Since I am free through grace, there is no law for me to keep! I can go on sinning! I am saved to sin!

It has been said that Christ is forever crucified between the two thieves of legalism and license. To this licentious notion Paul says,

> For you were called to freedom, brothers. Only do not use your freedom as an opportunity for the flesh, but through love serve one another (Galatians 5:13).

And this leads us to the section of Galatians we are considering today. J.C. Ryle, the old Bishop of Liverpool, spoke of "practical holiness."[3] And it is a term that I particularly like because I think it speaks to what Paul is dealing with here. Ryle was talking about practical holiness when he wrote,

> Sound Protestant and Evangelical doctrine is useless if it is not accompanied by a holy life.[4]

What does that mean? When I was a boy, there was one old gentleman who would walk the aisle of the church, in our tradition, just about every Sunday night. But this fellow had the worse mouth you ever heard! My Aunt Eva would tell me that it didn't matter about walking the aisle but about walking with Jesus. And that is what Paul is going to deal with here: practical holiness.

The Bible knows nothing of a feigned holiness. The Bible knows nothing of a holiness that is all show and conducts itself with theatrical folded hands and holier than thou manners of speech. I once had a speech teacher who told us that if she died before we did and she caught us using what she called a "holy clasp of the hands" or a "holy voice," she would come back to haunt us! She was referring to the tendency in clergymen to feign holiness in gestures as if that is revealing holiness in the souls. But the holiness of the Bible is born out of an encounter with the living Jesus Christ, and it produces a change in a man. Practical holiness is the spontaneous work of the Spirit in a man's life that gives him the "want to" to follow God.

---

[3] J. C. Ryle, *Practical Religion:Being Plain Papers on the Daily Duties, Experience, Dangers, and Privileges of Professing Christians*, New and improved ed. (Edinburgh: Banner of Truth Trust, 1998).
J. C. Ryle and Robert Backhouse, *Holiness* (London: Hodder & Stoughton, 1996).
[4] Mark Water, comp., *The New Encyclopedia of Christian Quotations* (Grand Rapids, MI: Baker Books, 2000), 478.

The Galatians needed it. And we need it. Here Paul lays out four aspects of practical holiness in the life of the true believer.

Practical Holiness Is Active

> But I say, walk by the Spirit, and you will not gratify the desires of the flesh (Galatians 5:16).

As John Stott puts it, "This section...is simply full of the Holy Spirit."[5] He is right. For holy living is not about our ability, but the Spirit's power and our prayer to Him to help us walk in His power. But what does it mean to walk by the Spirit? The NIV translation uses the term "keep in step with the Spirit," and I like it. J.I. Packer wrote a fine book about this command, using that phrase as the title.[6] It means that having come to Christ by the power of the Holy Spirit (and not through the law), you must not only yield to the Spirit passively but also seek His power actively, aggressively, or perhaps we should even say, intentionally.

Paul is making it clear that a man cannot just say, Well I have received the Holy Spirit and I have nothing more to do. I am positionally holy, and since it is all of the Spirit, I can finely rest. This is antithetical to the gospel.

This reminds me of the Quaker who said that in his service there is no call to worship at a particular time, per se. Because they want to yield to the Spirit, they simply assemble and wait until the Spirit moves. He told me that the Lord inevitably moved around 11:00 and pretty much released them around 12:00 or so. We both got a laugh out of that. I am not criticizing their way of doing things, but I do think that this is an example of a passive Christianity. We cannot just be passive in the Christian life. We must be active, but that activity can only be done by the work of the Spirit. We are to seek the Spirit. We are saved by grace, and grace produces a "want to," and we are called upon by God to act on that "want to" inside of us.

J.C. Ryle put it right:

> True holiness does not consist merely of believing and feeling, but of doing and bearing...Our tongues, our tempers, our natural passions and inclinations—out conduct as parents and children, masters and servants, husbands and wives, rulers and subjects—our dress, our employment of time, our behavior in business, our demeanor in sickness and health, in

---

[5] John R. W. Stott, *The Message of Galatians: Only One Way* (Leicester: Inter-Varsity, 1992).
[6] J. I. Packer, *Keep in Step with the Spirit* (Old Tappan, NJ: Flemming Revell, 1984).

riches and poverty—all, all these are matters which are fully treat by [the Biblical] writers.[7]

The way to keep in step with the Spirit is to keep in step with His Word, with Christ in the sacraments and through prayer. These are the ordinary means, or ways, that grow and allow the Holy Spirit to cultivate fruit in our lives.

For the man who says, Well, I cannot stop cursing. That is just the way I am. This passage says, Keep in step with the Spirit. The Spirit of God is clean and pure and transforms a man. Have you ever trusted in Christ? Yes, you say. Well, seek those things which are on high. Actively go to God and present your life and commit your heart and mind to follow Him with pure words.

For the woman who says, I cannot stop lashing out at my husband. I have tried. Keep in step with the Spirit. The Spirit calls you to surrender your life to your husband, to speak words of healing to him and about him, to lift him up, to esteem him, to honor him as Sarah honored Abraham. Make no excuses for the flesh, but actively seek God in His Word.

Next Sunday night is Communion, so this week prepare your heart by seeking the power of the Spirit in your life in this area. As you taste the bread, know that Christ was crushed under the teeth of your anger and your hatred and your disobedience to God. As you taste the cup, remember that Jesus shed righteous blood for your sin. And then pray. Pray often about your husband. Pray often about your own heart. And do not forsake the assembling of yourselfs together.

Actively seek Christ for your life. You were saved unto God. And if grace worked in you, grace will produce gratitude to God, and this gratitude will break your heart and conform you into the image of Jesus.

But we must be concerned about another aspect of practical holiness.

Practical Holiness Is Aware

> For the desires of the flesh are against the Spirit, and the desires of the Spirit are against the flesh, for these are opposed to each other, to keep you from doing the things you want to do. But if you are led by the Spirit, you are not under the law. Now the works of the flesh are evident: sexual immorality, impurity, sensuality, idolatry, sorcery, enmity, strife, jealousy, fits of anger, rivalries, dissensions, divisions, envy, drunkenness, orgies, and things like these. I warn you, as I

---

[7] Mark Water, comp., *The New Encyclopedia of Christian Quotations* (Grand Rapids, MI: Baker Books, 2000), 478.

> warned you before, that those who do such things will not inherit the kingdom of God (Galatians 5:17-21).

Fifteen works of the flesh are mentioned here. They involve a range of sins that spring from the poisonous sin nature of man, including sensual sins (immorality, impurity, sensuality), religious sins (idolatry, sorcery), sins against others (enmity, strife, jealousy, fits of anger, rivalries, dissensions, divisions), and sins against our own lives (envy, drunkenness, orgies). Then Paul adds, "and things like these." This tells us that his list is suggestive of what the sin nature produces. This is not a comprehensive list, but you get the picture pretty clearly.

Paul is telling the disciples at Galatia to watch. Jesus told his disciples to watch. To watch is to be aware—and in this case, to be aware of sin crouching at the door, to be aware of the struggle within. How did Paul put it in Romans 7?

> I do not understand what I do. For what I want to do I do not do, but what I hate I do (Romans 7:15, NIV).

We need to be aware of what the Bible teaches about human nature, or we will be caught off guard.

The Bible teaches that when Adam was placed in the garden, he was in a state of "possible to sin and possible not to sin."

> And the LORD God commanded the man, saying, "You may surely eat of every tree of the garden, but of the tree of the knowledge of good and evil you shall not eat, for in the day that you eat of it you shall surely die" (Genesis 2:16-17).

Adam chose to sin. And this cast mankind, federally through the headship of Adam, into a state of "impossible not to sin." This is the condition of the person without Christ, and this is what Paul is assuming in Ephesians 2:1 when he writes,

> And you were dead in the trespasses and sins (Ephesians 2:1).

This is the state of people without the power of the Holy Spirit in them. This is the state of people who have not been born again. They are powerless in the presence of sinful urges and are in rebellion against God unless they repent and receive Jesus Christ. They cannot do it without the power of God. But whoever cries out to God will be born again. Then, regenerated by the Spirit, that person returns to a state like that first state of Adam in the Garden: possible to sin and possible not to sin. This is assumed by Paul and all of the writers of the Bible when they address believers and say, as in Ephesians 4:1,

> I therefore, a prisoner for the Lord, urge you to walk in a manner worthy of the calling to which you have been called, (Ephesians 4:1).

There will come a time when we will be like Jesus—not possible to sin—but that is glorification and that is in heaven. But Paul is charging Christians who are faced with either giving in to the fleshly urges and temptations or deliberately walking in the Spirit (they may sin or not sin), to choose Christ.

So practical holiness is a result of the transformation of the human soul by Jesus Christ and produces a new way of life that reflects the life of Jesus. But that new way of life comes to man who is yet at war with the powers of sin. Practical holiness is aware.

We are aware but not defeated. For we see

Practical Holiness Is Abounding

It is in this passage that we see the context for the famous fruit of the Spirit passage.

> But the fruit of the Spirit is love, joy, peace, patience, kindness, goodness, faithfulness, gentleness, self-control; against such things there is no law (Galatians 5:22-23).

The fruit of the Spirit is, of course, the spontaneous produce of a soul that has been transformed by the Holy Spirit through faith in Jesus. Love is the fundamental force of all of this new life. It produces joy and peace, and this new inner man lives out patience, kindness, goodness to others. Faithfulness and self-control and gentleness now mark this new life. Paul says that "against such things there is no law." That is, a law is not needed to enforce the new life in Christ because such a life is of the Holy Spirit.

This morning as we witnessed the baptism of this little child, I can assure you that I do not need to say, "Now make sure you hold him tight! Now make sure you love him! Now you must be joyful that God has given you this child!" Of course not! Love and joy bubble up from the hearts of the parents because they are eternally grateful.

So, too, my beloved, works cannot produce what you really desire. What you want—freedom of the soul, love that controls your life, joy and peace—comes from gratitude to God for eternal life.

Only those who know that they are sinners and that Christ loves sinners and saves all who call upon Him can begin to have that love, joy, and peace.

Finally, practical holiness is not only active and aware and abounding, but also

Practical Holiness Is Applied

True holiness is a way of life, an ambition of the heart born of our gratitude to God for saving us, and this holiness is applied to real life. Thus Paul writes,

> And those who belong to Christ Jesus have crucified the flesh with its passions and desires. If we live by the Spirit, let us also walk by the Spirit. Let us not become conceited, provoking one another, envying one another (Galatians 5:24-26).

To draw on our opening illustration, the graffiti had to stop. Once Paul had dealt with the false teachers, he had to deal with those claiming grace but using it to sin. This cannot be. Grace produces love, not pride and division from others. Grace causes men to see themselves as God sees them; thus, they instinctively look upon others with love. But here, Paul mentions sins of conceit. Thinking too highly of one's self is an attack on grace. He mentions provoking, which comes from conceit. And he mentions envying, which speaks of Christians not looking to Christ but to individuals, to human achievement, to man-centered gifts. All of these sins had to be eliminated in the fellowship.

How would the bickering stop at Galatia? How would they erase the graffiti off the walls of Galatia? How must we apply the grace of God in our lives?

First, those who are Christ's will have "crucified the flesh with its passions and desires." What is it to crucify the flesh? This is a creative way of Paul saying, "False teachers told you that you had to circumcise skin in order to produce salvation. But outward religious ritual cannot produce holiness. The only way is to cut the flesh (the flesh is the sin nature which opposes God) through, not a legalistic circumcision of skin according to religion, but a crucifixion of the sin nature through the cross of Jesus."

To be crucified with Christ, to identify your life with the decisive event of salvation in which Jesus Christ bore the sins of sinners on that condemned cross, is how we are saved and how we are set free to follow Christ.

Second, Paul says that if we live by the Spirit, we must walk by the Spirit. There can be no talk of, He is my Savior but not my Lord. There can be no talk of a "higher life," an esoteric philosophical existence that is disconnected from the real life of following Jesus Christ through the everyday trials and tribulations of life. The grace-centered believer says, I am not my own. I have been bought with a price; therefore, out of gratitude for Your grace, I will walk with You.

Conclusion

That is practical holiness, a holiness produced by grace and forged in grace at the foot of the cross, a new way of life that is active, aware, abounding, and applied.

One of the darkest and saddest lives in English literature was that of Oscar Wilde. In a book I read recently entitled *The Unmasking of Oscar Wilde*,[8] the author shows how Wilde, out of a rebellion against the God who pursued him all of his life, virtually lived out the downward cycle of sin described in Romans 1:

> Claiming to be wise, they became fools, and exchanged the glory of the immortal God for images resembling mortal man and birds and animals and reptiles. Therefore God gave them up in the lusts of their hearts to impurity, to the dishonoring of their bodies among themselves, because they exchanged the truth about God for a lie and worshiped and served the creature rather than the Creator, who is blessed forever! Amen (Romans 1:22-25).

Oscar Wilde's true soul was thus masked for most all of his life by pretension. He pretended to be fanciful and free. He would write the witty *The Importance of Being Earnest* but could not learn the truth of the importance of being honest. Wilde was miserable and ran from God through drugs and sex and lies. His literary gifts brought him great fame and fortune, but his unbridled lusts destroyed him. He was finally unmasked in a most public trial that rivaled the O.J. Simpson trial of our era and was found guilty of the most deplorable acts of indecency. He went to prison, but once released, he begged on the streets of Paris and, like a slave to sin, returned to the life that had put him in prison. He was estranged from his wife and two sons for the rest of his life. But before he died, the God of grace from whom he had fled throughout all of his life, was there. This new book suggests how Oscar Wilde, the man who ran from God and who became a public disgrace, finally was gripped by the grace he had all of his life rejected. In the end, all he had was Jesus Christ. And his heart was changed. He was finally unmasked, and a new way of life was born only as he died.

You do not have to live the life of Oscar Wilde to find that grace which produces holiness. You can find the grace he found now. The joy he apparently knew for only a few months, you can know for the rest of your life.

---

[8] Joseph Pearce, *The Unmasking of Oscar Wilde* (San Francisco, CA: HarperCollins, 2004).

Wherever you are, a person needing to bring your life to the cross for the first time or the next time, you come just as you are without one plea—without a mask—and receive God's gift of grace through Jesus Christ who loved you and lived for you and died for you. Only in coming to Jesus Christ by faith, only by returning to the cross with your sins, will you ever take off the mask and be the man or woman God formed you to be.

Questions for Reflection

1. How is it that all theology must ultimately be practical? What does that mean to you?

2. If you agree with it, how do you see Paul promoting a practical holiness?

3. Go back and examine, in the text, what we find of the "Galatian graffiti" that was going on. In the context of accusations and parties, how did Paul handle the situation in regard to promoting the gospel? How is his approach similar or different to the way we should handle such factionalism in the church today?

4. What does it mean to keep in the step with the Holy Spirit? How may a Christian keep in step with the Holy Spirit?

5. How does the doctrine of God's grace lead to "practical holiness?"

6. How is it that a man like Oscar Wilde could desire the Christian life and yet miss it for so much of his life? Are there any correlations with those who try to break bad habits and can't? Explore this as you think about it.

7. How is it that the cross of Christ is the power for personal holiness?

Prayer

Holy God, I confess that for too long I have sought to please you through the flesh—through religious duty and moralism and turning over a new life and even pretending to be a person that I really know I am not. Forgive me. Empower me through open identification with Your cross, O Christ, so that what You require in Your law, You provide by Your Spirit. In this, may You be greatly glorified; and in Your holiness, my life is increasingly sanctified! I pray through the righteousness of Christ alone!

Amen.

"There is not a word in the Bible which is *extra crucem*, which can be understood without reference to the cross."

Martin Luther

"The church should be a community of encouragement."

Fred Catherwood

7

THE MARKS OF A GRACE-BASED CHRISTIAN COMMUNITY

Galatians 6:1-2, 6, 9-10, 14-18

F.F. Bruce called Paul of Tarsus the "Apostle of the Heart Set Free."[1] But Paul's heart set free always led him to give his life away to others. Just like Jesus. And so must ours. And the place where hearts are set free to serve is a place called the local church.

> Brothers, if anyone is caught in any transgression, you who are spiritual should restore him in a spirit of gentleness. Keep watch on yourself, lest you too be tempted. Bear one another's burdens, and so fulfill the law of Christ (Galatians 6:1-2).
>
> One who is taught the word must share all good things with the one who teaches (Galatians 6:6).
>
> And let us not grow weary of doing good, for in due season we will reap, if we do not give up. So then, as we have opportunity, let us do good to everyone, and especially to those who are of the household of faith (Galatians 6:9-10).
>
> But far be it from me to boast except in the cross of our Lord Jesus Christ, by which the world has been crucified to me, and I to the world. For neither circumcision counts for anything, nor uncircumcision, but a new creation. And as for all who walk by this rule, peace and mercy be upon them, and upon the Israel of God. From now on let no one cause me trouble, for I bear on my body the marks of Jesus. The grace of our Lord Jesus Christ be with your spirit, brothers. Amen (Galatians 6:14-18).

---

[1] F. F. Bruce, *Paul: Apostle of the Heart Set Free* (Grand Rapids, MI: Eerdmans, 1977).

THE ISRAEL OF GOD

The other day I was trying to check out in a grocery store. I noticed that a man was doing some shopping for his wife, probably just like I was. As he went to check out, he got in one of those lines labeled "10 items or less." I didn't count, but I figure he probably had, oh, say, 150 items! Well, the lady behind him let him have it!

"You are in the wrong line!" she screamed, as if he had just made it past airport security with a M-16 in his bag. The poor man looked slightly dazed by the woman's accusation and sheepishly got out of that line and got in line with me. I didn't have the heart to tell him that my line was 5 items or less!

Well, it's no fun to be in a place where you are not wanted.

Paul wanted Gentile believers to know that they were not in the wrong line. They had understood it right the first time. You are saved by God's grace through faith in Jesus Christ alone. Not through anything else. However, false teachers had told them, in essence, You are in the wrong line.

But you can never be in the wrong line if you are following Jesus. Wherever you come from, whatever you have done, whatever language you speak, you are in the right line, you are in the right place, if you are following Christ.

In Galatians 6:16 Paul calls such a people "the Israel of God." This is defiant language to not only rude, but wrong-headed teachers who mandated salvation by religious ritual. But "the Israel of God" also speaks to the fulfillment of God's promise that the covenant made with Abraham would extend to the whole world of men. And today the the Israel of God—made up of all nationalities, all races, all backgrounds, all colors, all socio-economic groups, males and females—represents a community of the free. These are the people who have trusted in Jesus Christ as Lord and Savior and who are in fellowship with one another through Him. These people are in the right line. And in Galatians 6, the Apostle applies the teachings about grace to the lives of this community.

There is much that we can learn about how authentic Christianity is really a community of the free. We may say this passage is about life in a grace-based community. What are the marks of this grace-based community? Looking at this chapter, there are three major marks of a grace-based community.

A Grace-Based Christian Community Is Marked by the Bearing of Burdens (Galatians 6:1-5)

The centerpiece of this section is Galatians 6:2.

> Bear one another's burdens, and so fulfill the law of Christ. (Galatians 6:2)

Law cannot save. That has been the proposition of Galatians. Only faith in the finished work of Jesus Christ saves. It is only out of a transformed life that a Christian is able, even wants, to follow God's law. And the way to fulfill that law is through burden bearing. Those who claimed that the law brought holiness should have known this because of the command in Leviticus.

> "'Do not seek revenge or bear a grudge against one of your people, but love your neighbor as yourself. I am the LORD (Leviticus 19:18, NIV).

And Jesus was teaching this when he gave the summary of the law.

> And he answered, "You shall love the Lord your God with all your heart and with all your soul and with all your strength and with all your mind, and your neighbor as yourself." (Luke 10:27)

When we are a community freed by God through faith in Jesus and marked by His grace, we will bear the burdens of others.

The specific context of this admonition to bear burdens is during the time when one is caught in a transgression. The Greek word here literally means to stumble, to fall. And Paul tells us that those who are spiritual—that is, those who are walking with the Lord and who are unhindered by such sin—should restore the one who has fallen. Paul says that we are to show gentleness; then, lest pride creep in, we are to remember that we too could fall into sin.

An airline company was disturbed over a high percentage of accidents, so they decided to eliminate human error by building a completely computerized plane. "Ladies and gentlemen," came a voice over the speaker during the initial flight, "it may interest you to know that you are traveling in the world's first completely automated and computerized plane. Now just sit back and relax because nothing can go wrong...go wrong...go wrong...go wrong..."[2]

The truth is, sometimes things can go wrong. Paul says that a grace-based community is a place that will catch you if you fall. A grace-based community listens to Paul say in Romans that, in fact,

---

[2] This illustration was used by David Curtis and may be found in his sermon at http://www.bereanbiblechurch.org/transcripts/topical/bearing_burdens.htm

> ... all have sinned and fall short of the glory of God, (Romans 3:23).

A grace based community listens to God in His Word in 1 John:

> If we say we have no sin, we deceive ourselves, and the truth is not in us. If we say we have not sinned, we make him a liar, and his word is not in us (1 John 1:8, 10).

We remember the words of James 3:2:

> For we all stumble in many ways... (James 3:2).

You see, what Paul is teaching these grace-needy people in Galatia and what God wants His people always to see is that we must reflect the gracious heart of a forgiving God towards sinners. The Psalmist writes of this burden-bearing God.

> Cast your burden on the LORD, and he will sustain you;
> he will never permit the righteous to be moved (Psalms 55:22).

Jesus is the beautiful incarnation of grace when we hear Him say,

> "Come to me, all who labor and are heavy laden, and I will give you rest. Take my yoke upon you, and learn from me, for I am gentle and lowly in heart, and you will find rest for your souls. For my yoke is easy, and my burden is light." (Matthew 11:28-30).

Don't you want to be that kind of church? This is an open call to people who have fallen in sin: Come home. This is a Biblical command for every believer here: Go and find a burden and bear it.

When I was a boy, I was climbing in a big old live oak tree that sat right behind the old tabernacle chapel down the road from my home. As I was climbing, I slipped and fell into the barbed wire below the tree. I was dangling, being held by my skin attached to the barbed wire, and was screaming through unbearable pain. By God's good providence, Brother DeValle, the lay preacher, was in the little chapel. He heard my screaming and came out and rescued me. It must have been a sight to see for Aunt Eva—Brother DeValle walking down the gravel road to our house, carrying me in his arms. He had blood all over him, but that old lay preacher would take his big old laborer hands and wipe my tears and hold me close as he carried me home.

If anyone falls, you are in the right place. If you scream out of your pain, we will hear you. You may be tangled up in a real mess, but in a grace-based community, someone will be there to help lift you out and to hold you and to carry you all the way home. That is why the church exits.

Find healing right here in our church. We want to minister to you in the name of Jesus Christ. We are sinners who have found forgiveness, and that which we have found, we want to extend to you.

A Grace-Based Christian Community Is Marked by Blessing Believers (Galatians 6:6-10)

Paul talks about how grace forges a community of grace in which believers intentionally go in search of others to bless. The core of this passage may very well be Galatians 6:9-10:

> And let us not grow weary of doing good, for in due season we will reap, if we do not give up. So then, as we have opportunity, let us do good to everyone, and especially to those who are of the household of faith (Galatians 6:9-10).

So everyone is to be blessed; that is, the church of Christ is to bring the grace of Christ to the whole world in intentional acts of mercy and compassion. But note that Paul says, "especially to those who are of the household of faith."

The church is a place marked by believers bringing blessing to other believers. This is a place to belong. This is a place to be family. This is a place to be accepted because Jesus Christ has accepted you.

Earlier in the passage, Paul shows that in the household of faith there are pastors, teachers, to be blessed. We read,

> One who is taught the word must share all good things with the one who teaches (Galatians 6:6).

My waistline demonstrates that since coming to First Presbyterian Church, we have learned you do that very well! But I want to honor Bob Venable today. He has not only been a great Clerk of Session, but he has blessed this pastor and teacher. Bob, of course, served through the three years of senior pastor vacancy before the Lord led me here. He was pretty tired by the time I showed up. He and many of you literally prayed me into this pulpit. But Bob told me that he would not give up his clerk's post until he felt I was settled. He walked with me, advised me, counseled me, led me, prayed for me, and held me through thick and thin. Training a preacher is hard! But Bob brought blessing to my life. In short, Mr. Venable modeled this passage. The one who is taught shared good things with the one who teaches.

And that is how we are to be to each other in this church.

Recently I heard a St. Peter joke. In this case, someone shows up at the gate in heaven. St. Peter says that he has searched the records to see if he has ever brought a blessing to anyone else. The man said, "Absolutely. In fact, I once blessed this lady who was in need. You see, I saw this oversized, overfed, tattooed, mean, grizzly bear bunch of leather-bound bikers who were hassling an old lady. I pulled over and went right up to the biggest one I could find. I got right in his face, and I pulled his nose ring right out of his nose just to get his attention. I screamed as loud as I could, 'Mr., if you are messing with this lady, you need to know that you are messing with me.'" St. Peter said, "That is an amazing act of bringing blessing to another. But I don't see it in your records. When did it happen?" The man replied, "About three minutes ago."

Bringing blessings to others can be a hard business. But there is a reward, and not just in heaven. In due season—a time known unto God—blessings bestowed will be blessings returned. That is the promise of the harvest.

Maybe today you can intentionally ask God to lead you to be a blessing to a believer right here. Maybe it is a visitor who needs to know that you will be here next week to be their friend. Maybe as you ask someone, "How ya doin'?" and you get an answer that they are going to have surgery this week, you can invite them to prayer—right where you are.

You see, this church has always been and must always be a grace-based fellowship where blessings abound. If you are without a place to call home, we welcome you here.

It would be a blessing.

A Grace-Based Christian Community Is Marked by Boasting in the Cross (Galatians 6:11-16)

My old professor, Dr. Robert L. Reymond, used to quote this passage in his theology class and say that all theology must lead to this verse:

> But far be it from me to boast except in the cross of our Lord Jesus Christ, by which the world has been crucified to me, and I to the world. (Galatians 6:14)

Anytime a first year seminarian got enough theology to be dangerous and to start thinking he had it all figured out, Dr. Reymond would tell us, "Brothers, if we believe that it is all of grace and not of man, then we have nothing to boast of. Never let theology become a source of pride. Rather, let it reduce you to being prostrate before Almighty God. Let it work in you humility and love and brokenness for your sins, passion for the lost, a heart for missions, and let it, above all, bring you back again and again to the cross of Christ."

Some years ago, one of my parishioners went to a seminar on how to grow churches. I am always interested in such titles because I always remember Jesus saying, "I will be build my church..." It is not a human thing to do. But I know what the consultants mean, so I don't push it! Well, anyway, this fellow came back and told us that the expert had said, "If you have a cross in your church, get rid of it. The cross doesn't really speak to the unchurched."

I think it speaks volumes. We had a cross. But we didn't get rid of it. And we never should. The cross is what we are all about. The cross conveys many truths.

The cross speaks of man's sin, of God's wrath against sin. But it also speaks of God's love and Christ's sacrifice for sinners. One of my favorite old hymns powerfully speaks to the centrality of the cross and how it is the thing in which we should boast:

> In the cross of Christ I glory,
> Towering o'er the wrecks of time,
> All the light of sacred story
> Gathers rounds its head sublime.
>
> Bane and blessing, pain and pleasure,
> By the cross are sanctified;
> Peace is there that knows no measure,
> Joys that through all time abide.

CONCLUSION

So we have learned that a grace-based church is a place where people bear burdens. Are you doing that? Are you praying for someone? Are you reaching out to another person to share your life with them? We have learned that a grace-based church is a place that blesses believers. Does that characterize your relationships here? Are you an encourager to others? Do you seek out opportunities to be a blessing? We have also learned that such a community boasts only in the cross of Jesus Christ. The teaching of grace in Galatians 6 leads us to see that it is all about Christ and His atonement for sin on the cross. I have nothing to boast of. I am not even here because I am smarter, holier, better, or anything else. I am here because of God's grace. And maybe I need to share that grace with another person.

Last week I came to church early to get ready for the early worship service. Something was wrong. Mr. Lewis Gross was not here. He was sick last week. Mr. Gross is a man who gets here early and prays with me. He joins others of us, and together we go into the prayer room and ask God's blessing on the day. We pray for Christ to be glorified in the services. We pray for those in need to be drawn here and that Christ will be lifted up and draw them to Himself. But as we go around, Mr. Lewis Gross always prays about the same thing, "Lord we pray for believers all over the world meeting like this. Bless them, Lord." I missed his praying that. I missed his praying that because his prayer reminds me that it is not just about me or about my church and my sermon and my life and my community. Mr. Gross' prayer leads me out of isolation and into community with Christians all over the world. His weekly passionate prayer reminds me that grace has set us free to be part of a world-wide, universal movement of sinners being saved by the life and atoning death of Jesus Christ.

As I complete this series on Galatians, it would be wrong for me to finish without an invitation for you to be a part of that grace place. Paul ends his letter with these words:

> The grace of our Lord Jesus Christ be with your spirit, brothers. Amen (Galatians 6:18).

His grace comes to all who repent of their sins and call upon His name by faith. It is not of works. It is all of grace. That is authentic Christianity. And it is absolutely free to all who call on the name of Jesus.

Questions for Reflection

1. In what way may we call Paul the "Apostle of the Heart Set Free"? If this could be an apt description of any believer, how are you living out your freedom?

2. Were Christians in Galatia being made to feel as if they were second-class citizens in the kingdom of God? If so, how and by whom? How is this possible in our fellowships today?

3. Who is the "Israel of God" according to Paul in Galatians 6:16?

4. How does the theological dogma of salvation by grace through faith in Jesus Christ relate to compassion in the local church or in a believer's relationships with others?

5. What are practical ways that Christians may show God's grace to the unbelieving world? How about to each other? Are the concepts of justice and mercy and hospitality unrelated to Biblical theology? How is justice related to God's grace?

6. How would you share the gospel of grace with someone who was seeking to please God through religious duty? How can the gospel of God's grace be shared while addressing the requirement of God's Law?

Prayer

Lord of grace, whose only begotten Son lived a perfect life to keep the law, and who died a sacrificial death to pay for my transgressions of the law, enable me, though Your Spirit, to daily embrace this gospel of grace. And lead me, O Christ, to the person you want me to meet this day, so that I may share the Good News of Jesus Christ that brings freedom to another. In Jesus' name I pray.

Amen.

Michael A. Milton

In 2001, Dr. Michael A. Milton was called as the pastor of the historic First Presbyterian Church of Chattanooga, Tennessee, the twelfth in 161 years. As senior pastor, he provides expository preaching, teaching, and worship leadership to a growing congregation of over 2,000. He also serves as staff leader to pastors, directors, and hundreds of volunteers in a multi-faceted ministry that includes a radio and television outreach, a vibrant departmental Sunday School ministry, an aggressive world missions program, a camping ministry, and an outreach to the nation through numerous local and national agencies and ministries. He can be heard on the *Faith for Living with Mike Milton* radio ministry in select regional markets of the United States and on the Internet at 1stpresbyterian.com. Dr. Milton is the author of the book *Leaving a Career to Follow a Call: A Vocational Guide to the Ordained Ministry*, as well as numerous popular and academic articles and published sermons in such periodicals as *Preaching Magazine*, *The Journal of the Evangelical Theological Society*, *The Christian Observer*, and *World Magazine*. He has been featured on national radio and television programs such as *Truths that Transform* with Dr. D. James Kennedy, *The Coral Ridge Hour*, and Moody Radio's *Money Matters*.

Prior to becoming Senior Pastor at First Presbyterian Church of Chattanooga, Dr. Milton served sixteen years in the business world and was also a top secret Navy linguist. He interned under D. James Kennedy at Coral Ridge Presbyterian Church and after seminary, planted two churches: Redeemer Presbyterian Church in Overland Park, Kansas; and Kirk O' the Isles Church in Savannah, Georgia. He also founded Westminster Academy Christian School in Overland Park and was the administrative head and a professor at Knox Theological Seminary. A graduate of Mid America Nazarene University (Kansas) and Knox Theological Seminary, in 1998 he earned a Doctor of Philosophy degree in theology and religious studies from The University of Wales (UK).

Dr. Milton's personal story of moving from orphan and prodigal son to understanding God's grace and receiving His adoption through Jesus Christ forms a frequent motif for offering Christ's healing to a broken generation. Often his sermons are illustrated with songs that he writes, sings, and performs with guitar.

In addition to his pastoral work, Dr. Milton holds a commission in the US Army Reserves as a chaplain, a ministry that he continues. Serving on several boards and active in a number of civic organizations, he also remains involved in preaching and teaching in churches, conferences, and seminaries. Mae and Mike are the parents of seven adult children and live with their ten-year-old son, John Michael, on Signal Mountain, Tennessee, where they are frequently found puttering in the garden.

www.ingramcontent.com/pod-product-compliance
Lightning Source LLC
Chambersburg PA
CBHW070934160426
43193CB00011B/1688